Wooing &
Winning
Business

To Judith,
a sister
who saup it with
heart.
♡ Spring

Wooing & Winning Business

The Foolproof Formula for Making Persuasive Business Presentations

Spring Asher
Wicke Chambers

JOHN WILEY & SONS, INC.

New York • Chichester • Brisbane • Toronto • Singapore • Weinheim

Copyright © 1997 by Chambers and Asher Speechworks.
Published by John Wiley & Sons, Inc.

Library of Congress Cataloging-in-Publication Data
Asher, Spring.
    Wooing & winning business: the foolproof formula for making
persuasive business presentations / Spring Asher, Wicke Chambers.
        p.   cm.
    Includes index.
    ISBN 0-471-14192-5 (alk. paper)
    1. Business presentations.   I. Chambers, Wicke.   II. Title.
HF5718.22.A84   1997
858.4'52—dc21   96-39234
                                                              CIP

Printed in the United States of America
10 9 8 7 6 5 4 3 2 1

To the families that support us . . .

The Speechworks family, the Chambers family, and the Asher family, especially Benjamin, Billy, Elliott, Rufus, Brandon, Adair, and Jack: The Next Generation.

Contents

Acknowledgments

"To do the common thing uncommonly well brings success."
John D. Rockefeller

As they say at the end of a television newscast: "Our thanks to the people who made this possible:"

Our media mentors at WXIA-TV, WSB-TV, and *The Atlanta Journal Constitution* who drilled us as television producers and columnists to give viewers and readers "news they can use."

Business book guru Jack Covert, president of Schwartz Business Books, who has been our coach in the world of business publishing.

The team at John Wiley & Sons, Inc., that creates books to help people develop careers. Our editor, Janet Coleman, for her insightful contributions.

Illustrator Bill Loring at Creative Services, Inc. for his imaginative artwork.

Our team at Speechworks: Pat Marcus Bocinec, who has worked on every version of this evolving manuscript, Speechworks coaches Schatzie Brunner, Lisa Hanson, Monica James, and Marilyn Ringo, whose contributions add to the quality of our programs and services.

Wooing & Winning Business

He stood erect. Their eyes met. His heart was
pounding as a shiver ran down his spine. His nostrils
flared and his skin glistened with the sweat of
anticipation. His body tensed. His lips parted and
in an excited voice he said, "Good morning ladies
and gentlemen of United Construction. Thank you
for this opportunity to speak to you today."

Male or female, if you've felt those shivering, quivering, heart-pounding symptoms, you must be making a business presentation.

When you're in hot pursuit of a dream client, a hunk of a sales contract, or the red-hot approval from a board of directors, you need a great opening line. You need to know what turns them on and what makes them say, "Yes! Yes! Yes!"

As executive producers of *Noonday,* a daily news and talk show on Atlanta's NBC affiliate, WXIA-TV, it was our goal to woo the viewers and win high ratings. How did we court the viewers and keep them tuned in?

We had to discover what turned them on, what made them beg for more, what appealed to their eye, and what created excitement and interest. By crossing our goal with the viewers' interests we were on target toward high ratings. We gave them news they could use. They gave us great ratings. It was a Woo-Win Strategy!

After producing more than 2,000 hours of programming, we can help you build ratings and revenues. This book offers you more skills, confidence, and joy than you are experiencing now in the business relationships you're flirting with. It shows you how to maximize the possibilities for presenting winning information to an audience of 1 or 1,000!

A wooing strategy is not about expensive restaurants and flowers. It's about discovering what your intended needs and proving you can deliver. This strategy makes decision makers feel understood. It calls for plain and simple reasons to make them confident and excited about the results you can achieve for them.

We make these skills easy to get your arms around. We'll show you how to make a business pitch that woos 'em and wins 'em—every time. It's easy, fun, and quick to show you what you have to gain, whether you're chasing a sale, flirting with a job interview, or pursuing board approval.

THRILLS THAT CHANGE YOUR LIFE

The object of your pursuits are many. You may want to:

✔ Sell an idea to management with confidence

✔ Have a roomful of clients take the right action

✔ Make a report that wins approval

✔ Motivate your team to get involved in a project

✔ Give a winning speech to peers or prospects

✔ Develop a relationship that becomes a sale

✔ Give a seminar that builds your reputation

✔ Beat out the competition in a competitive bid presentation

✔ Feel good about yourself and have others feel the same

In short, each of us *wants* and *needs* winning communication skills that help us reach our heart's desire. The Speechworks Formula works every time to assure you that you are on track whether you speak *impromptu* at a meeting or enter a *beauty contest* in competition for a major client. Just look at our record.

✔ Rick McCullough, president of Media Management Strategies, a 12-person media placement company, came to Speechworks—the company we run—because he was chasing a big account and didn't want to blow his 20-minute pitch to the CEO of a major retail furniture company.

    Four days after his coaching, he came charging back into our offices fired up about his recent success with the furniture chain. "It was the Speechworks Formula!" he exclaimed. "We won an eight million dollar contract!" Rick credited Speechworks for showing him the secret of good communication skills. He connected with the CEO.

✔ Like flowers and diamonds, dynamic and interesting visuals made a $100 million dollar difference for Robins & Morton, a 300-person construction company with headquarters in Alabama. The company had just been through the agony and frustration of losing four key presentation bids for hospital construction contracts.

"We've got the know-how and the experience," said Barry Morton, the incoming CEO. "What we don't have is strong communication skills."

Barry sent his three top presenters to Speechworks and two weeks later, armed with the Formula, confident body language, and visuals that told their story with eye-catching appeal, they aced their next three presentations and won bids worth over $100 million in construction contracts.

I'M JUST A PLAIN, ORDINARY PERSON. DO I HAVE WHAT IT TAKES?

We hate to speak in front of a group because we hate being evaluated. Even worse, we hate playing a game when we aren't sure what it takes to win. If you can answer the following questions, you have what it takes to woo and win:

Can you count to three?

Can you smile, make eye contact, look someone in the eye, and shake hands?

Can you stand balanced on both feet or sit forward in your chair?

Can you reach your hand forward and hold a gesture?

Can you take four or five steps in one direction and then three to four in another?

Can you speak loudly and softly, quickly or slowly?

Can you put your two lips together and pause for five seconds?

Fine, then you have the talent that is required to become a comfortable and capable communicator. Selling to one person or a group successfully is like talking to a good friend, only *bigger. Bigger* organization of thoughts, *bigger* voice, *bigger* energy, and *more* conviction.

ARE YOU CRAZY?
OF COURSE YOU'RE PERSUASIVE

Have you ever tried to talk a few friends into going to your favorite restaurant? You're pumped, powerful, and persuasive.

You begin by assuring them that they will love it, that it's the best southwestern food in town. You give tempting specifics about the hot and spicy tamales served with a special sauce. Then you drive the point home with evidence that the place has a great atmosphere. You paint pictures of good times and great eats. Your language is mouth-watering and your enthusiasm takes the lead. Slide that same energy, intensity, and enthusiasm into your business presentation and you're on a persuasive roll.

SURE, YOU CAN *FAKE IT TIL YOU MAKE IT*

We saw you do it at a party when a total stranger came bounding up to you calling you by name. You didn't have a clue as to who it was, but that didn't stop you from replying with great energy, "Hey, how in the world have you been?"

If you can fake a total blank, you can pull off a confident delivery with the same assured ease. The Speechworks *fake it til you make it* plan is designed to prove to you that even though you're sure everyone can see your knees knocking, your nerves won't show. The great epiphany in our workshops comes when nervous clients see their video tape and declare, "I didn't look nervous . . . even though I was a wreck!"

YOU'VE GOT THE GUTS

Just as the Wizard of Oz gave the lion a badge of courage, the Speechworks Formula offers you your own shot of courage.

It worked for Betty Lemmon. Hear her roar.

Dear Speechworks,

I didn't want to go to the Speechworks workshop and rescheduled twice. I was apprehensive. I was afraid that I would be intimidated by communicators who were better than me. Now, the day after the workshop I feel like I could conquer the world!

I was surprised by how comfortable you made me feel. The progression was so easy and changes happen to you without your even knowing it.

How in the world could you take someone who was petrified and have them *volunteer* to stand up and be *first* on the second day?"

HOW TO USE THIS BOOK

This book is designed to be a quick reference and guide to selling your ideas, your products, or yourself. If a major or minor presentation is coming up in two weeks, you may kick back and read the whole book. If your hands are already shaking and you're jetting off to woo a prospect, the following Quick Fix references will give you specific ideas of *what to do right now.*

In the Quick-Fix section in chapter 1, we'll show you how to organize your information and give a winning presentation when time is short.

Then we'll show you the strategy behind the Formula.

Short chapters and easy-to-find sections give you immediate choices. The fill-in sections will help you grow your repertoire of evidence and results-oriented stories. The table of contents is there to guide and comfort you.

Let us be your coaches. In our ten years as television producers, we never lost a guest, and we won six Emmys. During that time we learned that television is the role model for communicators today. You watch television anchors and personalities, and you know a good presentation when you see one. We'll give you the techniques that will keep your viewers tuned in and win you high ratings and career credibility.

Since leaving broadcasting, we have focused on business communication. In this book you will learn from us and from our clients at Turner Broadcasting, Georgia-Pacific, Holiday Inn Worldwide, BFI, Smith Barney, and others.

John Rasor, Forest Resources group vice president at Georgia-Pacific, said in a recent letter, "Our Forest Resource managers and foresters continue to gain confidence and communication skills working with you. Even better, they enjoy it." As Neil Williams, managing partner at Alston & Bird, Atlanta's largest law firm, wrote, "Thank you for making us better at what we do."

You *can* woo your listener.

PART 1

WOOING THE CLIENT

1
The Quick Fix
Presentation Helper

I f your palms are sweaty and you feel the hot breath of a deadline on your neck, the Speechworks coach is here to help you woo your listener. The coach will guide you step-by-step to an effective, well-organized presentation using the Speechworks Formula. Then there are hot tips on how to come across with confidence and conviction with all the right moves.

When the pressure's passed, leisurely read the book. When it comes to giving business presentations, each of us is a work in progress. This Quick Fix Presentation Helper is the first step.

HOW TO ORGANIZE YOUR PRESENTATION: THE SPEECHWORKS FORMULA

1. TELL 'EM THE "WHAT'S IN IT FOR THEM": PREVIEW
   The Hook: Grab the listener's attention with one of the following: a story, personal example, expert testimony, analogy, quote, statistic, or a question.

Message Objective/Benefit Statement: Cross your goal with the need of your listener.

Preview your three points.
1.
2.
3.

2. TELL 'EM: THE BODY OF THE PRESENTATION
Make each point and illustrate it with evidence. Evidence *SPEAKS* to the need of the listener: Stories, Personal examples, Expert testimony, Analogies, (K)quotes, Statistics, and facts.

Point 1.
Evidence:

Point 2.
Evidence:

Point 3.
Evidence:

Each point may have subpoints.

3. TELL 'EM WHAT YOU TOLD 'EM: RECAP

Recap Message Objective/Benefit Statement:

Recap your three points.
1.
2.
3.

Wrap Up: Call to action, ask for the order, give a final piece of evidence.

THE SPEECHWORKS FORMULA: SAMPLE PRESENTATION

1. TELL 'EM THE "WHAT'S IN IT FOR THEM": PREVIEW

 The Hook: There are 33 million business presentations given every day according to *Business Week* magazine. That presents the possibility for a lot of boring!

 Message Objective/Benefit Statement: Invest in communication skills to woo your prospects and win business. . . . Read *Wooing & Winning Business.*

 Preview your three points.
1. Build your case persuasively by using the Speechworks Formula.
2. Present with conviction.
3. Use the Formula to win in all types of business presentations.

2. TELL 'EM: THE BODY OF THE PRESENTATION

 Point 1. Build your case persuasively by using the Speechworks Formula.
Evidence: Mark Abkemeier, Blue Cross–Blue Shield sales executive said, "We increased our HMO sign ups from 35 percent to 72 percent by using the Formula. The examples were so powerful, buyers couldn't say no."

 Point 2. Present with conviction.
Evidence: 55 percent of the impression you make is in your presence; 38 percent is in your voice energy, according to UCLA social scientist Dr. Albert Mehrabian. This book shows you specific techniques that make you look like you're in control even when you don't feel like it.

 Point 3. Use the Formula to win in all types of business presentations.
Evidence: The Speechworks Formula, when used in a team presentation by Arthur Andersen LLP, gave them a major victory. They took a 20-year client away from a competitor.

THE SPEECHWORKS FORMULA:
SAMPLE PRESENTATION (*Continued*)

3. TELL 'EM WHAT YOU TOLD 'EM: RECAP

 Recap Message Objective/Benefit Statement: Invest in communication skills to woo your prospects and win business. . . . Read *Wooing & Winning*.

 Recap your three points.

1. Build your case persuasively by using the Speechworks Formula.

2. Present yourself with confidence.

3. Use the Formula to win in all types of business presentations.

 Wrap Up: call to action, ask for the order, give the final piece of evidence. You can be a winner, too. Wayne Gordon, executive vice president of Robins & Morton, said, "In the past three months, since we started working with Speechworks *Wooing & Winning* Formula, we have won over $100 million dollars in building contracts." Let *Wooing & Winning* help you grow.

A SESSION WITH THE
SPEECHWORKS COACH

By now you've gathered the information relevant to your presentation. Fill in the Formula by answering the Speechworks coach's questions. Woo your listeners by putting them at the center of your presentation. Focus on the listener's needs and interests and you'll begin a long-term relationship that builds business.

* *By* investing in communication skills, *you will* win business.
** (Action phrase): *Invest* in communication and *win* business. . . .

WE'RE ON A ROLL! WE'RE INTO THE BODY OF YOUR PRESENTATION. GIVE EVIDENCE TO PROVE POINT 1.

1. _____
_____
_____

NOW POINT 2.

2. _____
_____
_____

ONE LAST DECISION. EVIDENCE FOR YOUR THIRD POINT.

3. _____
_____
_____

GREAT STUFF! NOW THE RECAP.

MO _____
1. _____
2. _____
3. _____

WE'RE ALMOST DONE. TO OPEN, WE NEED A HOOK THAT GRABS YOUR LISTENER.

TO HOOK 'EM I GUESS I COULD ASK A QUESTION _____ OR START WITH MY GREAT STORY ABOUT _____ _____

NOW, TO CLOSE, USE A WRAP-UP STORY OR CALL TO ACTION.

I'LL END WITH THE ANSWER TO THE QUESTION, _____ OR MY FAVORITE STATISTIC _____ AND THEN I'LL ASK FOR THE ORDER.

YOU'VE DONE IT! YOU HAVE A LISTENER-CENTERED PRESENTATION. *IT'S A WINNER!*

PRESENTATION POWER

Come before your listener wearing boots and spurs, not bedroom slippers.

✔ Project energy in your pace and in your presence

✔ Stand balanced on the balls of your feet—feet eight to twelve inches apart

✔ Lift your chest

✔ Hold your head up

✔ Relax your arms at your sides
This is your home base, neutral position
(See chapter 7.)

Make eye contact to build relationships.

✔ Talk one-on-one to individuals in a group

✔ Give each listener a whole thought or idea
(four to six seconds)
(See chapter 8.)

Don't stand there like a tree.

✔ Use your whole body to reinforce the message

✔ Reach forward, toward your listener

✔ Hold gestures firmly so not to distract from your message
(See chapter 9.)

Add spice.

✔ Change the pace in your voice; speak loud, soft, fast, and slow

✔ Articulate. Open your mouth, enunciate to be understood
(See chapter 10.)

Use "the pause that refreshes"

✔ Pause to let your ideas sink in

✔ Pause to replace the *ehs* and *ers*

✔ Pause for confidence
(See chapter 11.)

2
What Turns Them On

What turns on your listener? Is it red-hot numbers, fast-paced stories, or statistics that sizzle? Show listeners what they gain by buying your product, approving your plan, or hiring you, and you get the results you want.

Different listeners have different needs. The CFO (chief financial officer) needs to know, "How will it save or make money?" The user of your ideas will want to know, "How will it make my job easier?" Say you need a new computer and your boss sees flying dollar signs. Say, "A new computer will save us time and money," and you will be given permission to prove it.

Make your listener the centerpiece of your presentation. Focus on his or her own special motivation. Advertisers know that a teen will buy the toothpaste that promises kissing-sweet breath, while the parent wants the one that prevents cavities.

All listeners wear a headset tuned into their favorite radio station, WII-FM, *what's in it for me?* When you tell them the benefits up front, you keep them tuned in and ready to hear you prove it.

KNOW YOUR LISTENER

> **"You can't sell 'em if you don't tell 'em."**

Fit your message to the listener's needs and chart a course that will take you where you want to go.

Columbus did it and so can you. "Legend has it that before Columbus met the King and Queen of Spain, navigational experts in Spain and Portugal had recommended against backing his unusual proposals to reach the Far East by sailing west," said Patricia Ward Brash, Miller Brewing Company's director of communications, in a communication skills presentation.

But Columbus understood the art of persuasion. He knew of Queen Isabella's wish to win more converts to her religion, so he told her of the masses of people in the Orient. He knew that King Ferdinand wanted to expand Spain's commercial power so he talked to him of the gold and spices awaiting in the East.

Columbus sold his idea based on each listener's interest and got the financial backing he needed. You can be just as persuasive no matter what your goal.

HOW DO YOU ASSESS YOUR LISTENER?

Do your homework. Subscribe to a prospect's trade journals for insight into their hot issues of concern. Read annual reports, research background information in newspapers and magazines. Get a copy of the organization's newsletter and find out what's hot and who's news in the workplace. Turn a key executive into an insider coach or take a friendly employee to lunch.

Bob Hope, comedian and longtime wartime entertainer of troops stationed around the world, knew how to woo and win his listeners. His staff researched the names of key soldiers, knew details of each camp, and the personal characteristics of commanders. He surprised, complimented, and built a kinship with the troops wherever he entertained. He knew that there are two radio stations on every listener's dial. In addition to WII-FM, consider the station, MMFG-AM, (*make me feel good about myself*).

After gathering background information, vital statistics, and determining the hot buttons and hot issues of the listener, you're ready to put the Formula into action. Turn this information into a motivating theme with three compelling points. Then gather convincing evidence that makes them eager to say *yes!*

> **"MMFG-AM:**
> **Make Me**
> **Feel Good**
> **About Myself"**

RECAP

MO: Tell your listeners the benefit up front to keep them interested.

→ Know your listeners' goals and objectives.

→ Focus your message on the benefit to the listeners: WII-FM.

→ Make them feel good about themselves: MMFG-AM.

3

The Formula:
Getting to
Yes, Yes, Yes!

KI.S.S. and tell: *Keep it simple, speaker,* and *tell* the benefit of tuning into your information. Business presenters and their listeners need a structure in order to create ties that bind. The Speechworks Formula accomplishes these two goals:

1. It makes it quick and easy for presenters to organize their information.

2. It makes it quick and easy for listeners to follow, file, and act on the speaker's information.

The following shows you how to use the Formula in detail.

TELL 'EM WHAT'S IN IT FOR THEM: PREVIEW

The Hook

The *Hook* is the grabber, the headline, the heart-stopping fact that gets the listener's attention.

Hook 'Em with a Gee Whiz Fact

A recruiter speaking to candidates for a sales position begins the presentation with, "$100,000,000 ... $100,000,000. That is the amount of money the people I recruited brought into our firm in the past year!" That gee whiz fact offered great sales possibilities for people looking for a job. The group wanted to hear more.

Hook 'Em with Humor

Frank Capiello, financial investment advisor and regular on TV's *Wall Street Week,* spoke after a recent stock market slide and got a laugh and our interest by opening with the comment, "In the stock market we used to be bulls and bears. Now we're all chickens!"

Don't waste time prattling on about "how appreciative you are to be there." Hook 'em with a gee whiz fact:

There are 33 million business presentations given every day, according to *Business Week* magazine.

Or ask a question relevant to your information:

How many of you would like to win the lottery?

Stories, personal examples, analogies, quotes, statistics and facts, and questions can grab your listeners' attention.

Your hook
Use a story, personal experience, expert testimony, analogy, quote, statistic, or a gee whiz fact to grab your listener.

_____

_____

_____

_____

After the Hook, you can say, "Good afternoon, I'm so glad to be here with you today."

Lisa Petty went for it. She was given the challenge to report to the executive committee on the telecommuting program initiated in her division at Equifax, the Fortune 500 data resource company.

Rather than beginning with an explanation of telecommuting, she led off with the story of Fred Campbell, a 56-year-old sales executive who violently resisted the change to working at home. She spoke of his metamorphosis from a reluctant

Hook 'Em with a Personal Connection

Tell a story that ties you to the life of the listener and breaks down barriers.

Madison Reilly, business consultant with Kurt Salmon Associates, spoke to retail executives on the changing needs of the American shopper. He spoke of the needs of his working wife in contrast to the buying style of his mother twenty-five years ago. His story showed his relationship to the listener and his awareness of their retail customers' problems.

Use History to Hook 'Em

A CPA with a Big Six accounting firm opened his presentation to his client by saying, "In 1987 it was said that Dow would probably reach 1000 by the year 2000 and here we are in 1995 and the Dow is almost at 5000. By thinking beyond people's expectations, we tripled your profit margins and delighted your shareholders."

Hook 'Em with a Common Cause

Before the Class Day Program at the Harvard graduation, Hank Aaron struggled to determine an opening for his address on personal responsibility. It was the same day his friend Mickey Mantle underwent surgery. As a personal response, he asked the group to join him in a prayer for his colleague and friend. The prayer united the group.

telecommuter to a convert singing the praises of his new independence. The result of change increased his sales productivity by 10 percent.

She hooked her audience, then inspired them with the step-by-step success of this test effort. Her credibility soared in front of the top corporate officers.

Message Objectives

Here are a few sample message objectives. The listener's benefit is italicized.

QRS45 computer *will improve your office efficiency and save your employees hours of paperwork.*

Let's see how this investment package *will help you achieve the long-term returns you want without undue risks.*

Adopt the new marketing plan and *insure visibility and profitability of the firm and our partnership.*

Know your competition as well as you know yourself and *get an edge over the other competitors.*

By working together for a master plan *we will create a strong identity for our businesses.*

The Message Objective

Here's where you sell your listeners on what's in it for them. This is the most critical factor in being persuasive. We feel that every presentation is meant to persuade. Even in an FYI (for your information) presentation the listener must be sold on the value of the information in making future plans and decisions.

If your Message Objective (MO) strikes the right notes, your listener will hang on your every word. If not, your listener may say, "So what," "No way," or tune out listing their objections.

Your MO

By _____ you will _____.
    (*your goal*)   (*listener's benefit*)

Example:
By changing to a team strategy your organization will be more productive.

Begin the statement with an active verb to add more impact:

Change to a team strategy and be more productive.

Three Points

Next, motivate your listeners with a quick preview of the points that support your MO. These are the points that will convince the audience you can deliver on what you promise. In this part of your presentation, preview the points so the audience knows what to expect. It's like the tease before the six o'clock news.

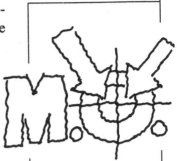

(MO)   "Stay tuned for the latest developments. Channel 11 puts you in the know.

(Preview)   In tonight's news, we'll cover the fraud story at City Hall, murder in the outskirts of downtown, and we'll go live to the birth of twin pandas at the zoo."

Why just three points?

Listeners, buyers, decision makers can't remember more than three clear, compelling messages. Forget eight, overloading points. Listeners simply can't store that volume. Simplify to succeed.

Having trouble getting your points down to just two or three? Do a brain dump. Write down all the points that come to mind and then group them into three categories with subpoints. This will help you identify which reasons are most important to your listener.

If you insist that you have ten points or more, change your mind. Speakers are like pitchers full of information, raring to pour all they know into the listener. Listeners, on the other hand, are like six-ounce cups. They can only hold so much.

The Formula works in every communication situation from a phone call to a sales call. In a report meeting, you can be instantly ready to make a presentation by building your points on the two to three questions your listeners may have.

(MO)   "Let me explain the progress of our division so that we can make changes needed to insure our growth.

(Preview)   The three questions on your mind
are: What is our employee retention
rate? "What are our costs?" and
What are our profits for the
quarter?"

Making Your Points

In a one-on-one sales presentation

Open with small talk (the Hook), which could be
anything from seeing a trophy and inquiring about
the prospect's interest in rowing, to acknowledging
the company's latest success featured in the newspaper. Then set the scene with an MO and three
points.

Example:

MO: By meeting today, we can see if our widgets
will save your operators time and money. I'd like to:

→ Ask you about your situation in relation to pro-
duction

→ Show you how our widgets work for organiza-
tions like yours, and

→ See if there's a fit

When you want to convince a friend to go to a movie:

MO: "To Wong Foo, Thanks for Everything, Julie
Newmar" was a funny movie.

→ You'll laugh and relax.

→ Wesley Snipes and Patrick Swayze are outrageous characters.

→ These big-city characters bring excitement to
small-town life.

Put your points in order, with the most important in the first or last position. "Research shows that jurors remember best what is said first and last," commented University of Georgia law professor Ron Carlson, in a *USA Today* article. This format works for every listener. Bury your weak point in the middle.

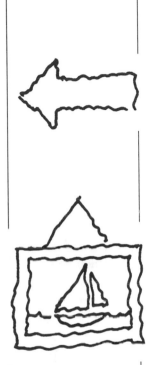

TELL 'EM: MAKE A POINT AND ILLUSTRATE IT

What does it take to build a fire under that Fortune 500 beauty with the knockout purchasing power to buy your product? How can you accomplish this in less than 30 minutes? Think *S.P.E.A.K.S.:* Stories, Personal experiences, Expert testimony, Analogies, (K)Quotes, and Statistics and gee whiz facts. Supporting evidence builds your credibility. This lineup speaks to the interest and heart of the listener. The specifics help you:

✔ Make your case

✔ Differentiate yourself from the competition

✔ Make your points memorable

The Evidence!

Build a war chest of case studies, stories, gee whiz facts, and statistics that you can access quickly to showcase your own successes and give support for your information. Take each point stated in the Preview and back it up with evidence.

Dale Carnegie said that the messages of his book, *How to Win Friends and Influence People,* could have been written in 1½ pages. The other 230 pages gave stories and evidence that proved the points he wanted to make.

We held a workshop for 30 sales executives at Shaw Industries. During the group presentation we asked for examples of customer successes to illustrate the points they wanted to make. It was a struggle initially. They weren't accustomed to using examples. They did not understand that a hotel manager would rather hear examples of how other hotel owners had benefited by using Shaw carpeting than a string of general statements that could be made by any competitor: quality, fade-proof color, value, on-time delivery.

When we left, two hours later, we had more than 30 different customer success examples that backed up points like quality or value. The group was amazed at the variety of examples it shared and determined to use them in future presentations.

Watch the television news to see illustrations in action. NBC anchor Tom Brokaw gives the Preview, "Let's look at Perostroika Pizza, the hottest new American enterprise on the streets of Moscow." He sends it to the reporter in the field who reviews it and tells 'em.

✔ *"The people love it."* Video shows man taking bite who says, *"Delicious."*

✔ *"It makes money."* Video shows U.S. owner cutting ribbon and giving projected first year's profits.

✔ *"It's fast."* Video shows people in line waiting for slow-cooking shashlik.

Examples, Evidence Document Success

Evidence makes presentations more interesting. Build mental pictures and invite the listener to identify with the problem and the success your company has achieved for others.

Billy McElroy, a project manager for Atlanta's Hardin Construction Company, was in a pitch for new business. Safety was a key factor, and, rather than make a series of statements about their safety program (which every other company could also make), he told a story about how he had stolen an idea from Ohio State football coach Woody Hayes to improve the safety on his construction projects.

"Hayes put a decal on the helmet of players who achieved certain goals. It was a visual motivator." McElroy explained how he used the same reward system on his subcontractors' hard hats when they achieved safety goals. This made the importance of safety on the job visually evident every day.

He showed the Hardin helmet with its safety decals to the prospective buyers, he demonstrated that the safety program was in place, and painted a picture the buyers weren't likely to forget. The rest of the story is that Hardin landed the contract!

Rev up your credibility and paint pictures that stick like glue in the minds of your buyers.

Build Your Evidence

Your evidence can be as long as a demonstration or as short as one sentence. Another contractor proved his company's quality work by saying, "After Hurricane Andrew came through Florida, our homes were the only ones left standing." Evidence S.P.E.A.K.S. to the need of your listener.

Stories: Relate to the interest that will build a connection between you and your listener. Use a war story to show how you or a member of your company handled or survived a tough situation.

_____

_____

Use a story from history to prove a point. "It took one hundred years to get a telephone on every desk. In only ten years, cellular phones have achieved the same market penetration."

_____

_____

> **"**The secret of *60 Minutes* success is very simple. . . . Tell me a story. Even the people who wrote the Bible knew that when you deal with the issues, you tell stories. The issue was evil; the story was Noah.**"**
>
> —Don Hewitt
> Executive Producer
> *60 Minutes*

Personal experiences: Share yourself in a presentation. It humanizes your information. It lets the listener *in* and helps you to build relationships. When you mention your hometown or your school, you build opportunities to connect. When a speaker relates a struggle overcome, listeners relate to their own personal struggles. When we relate our experiences as television producers with Ted Koppel or Jay Leno it adds to our credibility.

Expert testimony: Cite an expert to add credibility to your information. Explain who your expert is to increase your credibility. Frank Cappiello is a financial expert often seen on *Wall Street Week.* As a speaker he advises, "Never make more than three points in a presentation." His expertise reinforces our three-point philosophy.

Analogy: Find a likeness between unlike things. "The cleanup of the *Valdez* oil spill was so enormous that it was like trying to empty a bathtub with a cotton swab." Use analogies to create instant snapshots of your information. Sports and animals are common visual analogies.

(K)Quotes and Axioms: Some sayings just hit the mark. In setting your goals, you might quote Steven Covey, "Begin with the end in mind."

Statistics and gee whiz facts: Statistics are the most common and least memorable type of evidence. Talk about statistics as simplified relationships, not a series of charts and numbers. In a discussion of inflation, compare the cost of a loaf of bread 20 years ago with the price today. Round off all numbers. If you need to go into statistical detail, hand out materials *later.*

Make the statistic memorable. An acre is 43,650 square feet. Visualizing a quarter- or a half-acre lot is difficult for most people. Explain that an acre is the size of a football field without the end zones and everyone will get the picture.

Does the Evidence Pass the "So What?" Test?

Make sure your illustration is relevant to the listener. If the decision makers on an architectural project don't need a parking deck, don't ramble on about the awards your firm has won for innovative parking designs. It's an irrelevant, "so what?" statement. Stick to what's important to the buyer or show how the solutions on the parking deck relate to a problem they have.

Edit your information to essential points by asking, "What does this mean to the buyer?" Each time you add a point or a story, determine if it adds something of value to their file drawers or just clutters and crams an already overstuffed filing system.

The "so what" test keeps the focus on the news your particular audience can use. It eliminates *noise pollution,* irrelevant information that causes static and interrupts buyers' reception.

MAKE IT MEMORABLE

In our workshop, clients play the *Evidence Game* to show the value of stories. We present a list of words. After showing them and reading them aloud, the group is asked to write what they remember.

The exercise is repeated with a second set of words. This time, the random list is connected with a story. The scores double and triple from an average of 8 points the first time to 32 the second time. Participants can't believe how the addition of a story increases their ability to recall the random words.

Be Specific: Avoid Wandering Generalities

We call it the *People* Magazine/*National Enquirer* philosophy of presentation. The success of *People, Vanity Fair,* and the *National Enquirer* proves that people want to know the details. Be a reporter and tell the who, what, why of your story. Name names. Replace the anonymous *a man* or *someone* with the names of clients or the industry they represent. Personalize when possible to make your message more engaging. Use vivid language.

Would the server tempt you more with a suggestion of "a slice of chocolate cake" or "a mouth-watering piece of chocolate cake topped with fresh-picked raspberries and a scoop of French vanilla ice cream"?

Use Humor

"Humor is the shortest distance between two people," says comedian Victor Borge. *Funny* is saying the unexpected. Jokes are funnier if you make them your own. We feel that starting with a canned joke is out!

Collect your own stories. Steal funny newspaper headlines or phrases from a coworker or talk-show host Jay Leno and put your own twist on them. Keep your stories short and practice in front of your family—they'll let you know how you're doing.

The secret to using humor is not to pause for the laugh. If it doesn't come, keep right on going. If it does, pause and enjoy.

TRANSITIONS

Make your information memorable by making it easy for the listener to follow. As you move through the presentation, complete each point before you introduce the next subject.

"We have talked about the PGA *tournaments* (*point one*). Now let's talk about the *players* (*point two*). . . .

We have talked about PGA *tournaments* (*point one*) and the *players* (*point two*). Now let's talk about the *value of sponsorship* (*point three*).

This gives you a smooth transition and keeps your listener hanging on every word.

Longer presentations have points and subpoints. Preview each point at the beginning and take the listener through the subpoints. Give a brief recap and transition to the next point. This may sound repetitive, but it keeps the listener focused. In a presentation, unlike a book, listeners can't go back and check what they missed.

KEEP IT JARGON-FREE

Woo with simple, easy to understand words that build relationships. Avoid doublespeak as if your cash flow depended on it.

> ### How Long?
>
> Follow FDR's sage advice, "Be sincere. Be brief. Be seated." Shorter is better. The Formula will help you control your time. With an outline of just three main points you will be able to give your presentation in three minutes, thirty minutes, or three hours. The Formula works like an accordion and expands or contracts to fit time changes.

Greta Van Susteren, CNN's on-air legal analyst during the O.J. Simpson trial, had the job of telling those of us without law degrees what was going on. The jury wasn't sequestered, she said they were "cooped up." The defense didn't present evidence; it "came out swinging."

Language That Tries to Impress Fails to Connect

A financial consultant presented a plan to manage the portfolio for a group of surgeons. His plan overflowed with insider financial language. He drugged the medical doctors with money management jargon.

Did these brilliant surgeons buy into the plan? Did they trust what they could not understand? Could they ask questions without exposing their limited financial expertise?

No way. Who got the account? Another broker; one who asked questions, determined their concerns, and used language that connected with easy to understand examples. His easy to understand plan showed them how to grow their investment over time, save on taxes, and have the funds to enjoy their retirement. He set them up to be comfortable asking questions.

Doublespeak Is a Threat to Your Credibility

Doublespeak breeds distrust and creates suspicion of you and your message. An accountant from a power company objected to our plea for a simple message. He said, "When I speak to the mayors of these cities and tell it simply, they don't see the value of my expertise." . . . Hmmm.

Even if your listeners are aware of the language of your industry, an uncommon term can distract from the flow of information when the listener has to stop and translate.

Simplicity Increases Clarity

Connect with your listener. James Hume, speech coach and expert on Winston Churchill, makes the point, "Churchill didn't say, 'Hostilities will be engaged in the coastal perimeter.' He said, 'We shall fight them on the beaches.' " Fight jargon, bureaucratese, and pompous language on your own presentation beaches.

TELL 'EM WHAT YOU JUST TOLD 'EM: RECAP

Conclude with Conviction

Many speakers don't end a presentation, they just quit. It's like dinner without dessert; it's like a great date without a goodnight kiss. Other speakers seem to jerk to a conclusion like a teenager learning to drive a stick shift car: They come close to putting on the brakes and then lurch forward with just one more thought. Then there are those who never seem to find the end, who go past the time limit and wear out their welcome and their listeners.

After you have made the three points start putting on the brakes. "In conclusion," "finally," or "to wrap up" signals your listeners to listen up, the end is coming.

There are two parts in a strong conclusion. The first is to recap what's in it for them. The second is to give a wrap-up story, present the call to action, or ask for the business.

Recap to Increase Recall

You've taken the listener around the bases, one, two, and three. But you won't score if you don't bring the message home. Repeat your main benefit (the MO) and key points. For example:

(MO)	"Today we've focused on the importance of good communication skills to give your company the winning edge.
(Key points)	We've touched on three key areas:

→ How to focus on the interest of the listener

→ How to build your case persuasively, and

→ How to deliver it with confidence."

This short recap pulls it together for the listener and gives you a *solid ending.*

As the speaker, you may think you are being too repetitive. Although you hope that the listener's mind never wanders, the truth is that listeners *do* mentally fade in and out. The Recap is the final step in speeding up the decision making process. It increases and simplifies recall. As a result, you get to Yes! Yes! Yes! faster.

Get Listener Focused

Many people conclude a sales pitch or a motivational talk with a focus on, "We can. . . ." or "We will. . . ." Change that to, "*You*" or "*Your company* will get on-time delivery at an affordable price." This puts your listeners and their needs at the centerpiece of your wrap-up.

USE A WRAP-UP STORY AND THEN ASK FOR THE ORDER

In television, newscasters use a kicker story to wrap up. This is a story, gee whiz fact, or example that gives the viewer a smile or something to think about. When you're wooing a prospect, you need more. You need to let them know you want their business. The wrap-up story pulls it together and gives you an opportunity to ask for the order.

When the director of Investor Relations for a $2 billion company made her presentation for investors, her wrap-up story reminded them that each time their CEO promised specific results in three successive five-year plans, he delivered. "It meant a 20% return to you, the investors." They were so impressed by the promises he kept, they told her he was a rare corporate executive who always delivered.

Wrap Up with a Gee Whiz Fact

Example: Carr Lucas, the benefits manager at a large corporation, ended a presentation explaining that the cost of benefits would go up in the organization. He wrote these numbers on the board:

1.8

365,000

1,100

He said, "1.8 pounds is the weight of the baby my assistant delivered last year. $365,000 is what it cost the company to get that baby healthy and home. But the family only paid $1,100. So you see, although the cost of benefits is going up, we're going to be there when you need us." The story brought the presentation to a caring conclusion.

Don't Be Afraid to Show Heart

It was difficult to convince the members of a team at a Big Six accounting firm to use a personal story as their wrap-up. Like many business people, they thought it was unprofessional to use the human element to pitch the business.

They had made the short list and were making an oral presentation to a major city hospital. The firm had an unusual experience with the institution. In the past year, two of their partners had been hit in a random street shooting and were immediately rushed to this hospital.

After recapping the presentation, the team recounted how everyone in the hospital from the attending physicians and scrub nurses in surgery to the aides on the floor had given their all to the firm's partners and members of their families. The lead partner promised to treat their responsibilities to the hospital with the same care that had been given to their colleagues. They were awarded the account.

In a business competition, all of those who make the final pitch can do the job. What can you say that lets the decision makers know that you will go the extra mile for them?

IT CAN'T BE THIS EASY

A lawyer in our workshop came up to us after the first day and said, "People faced with any kind of presentation think they have a complex problem so they look for a complex solution. The Speechworks Formula makes it simple. It's quick to learn, easy to implement."

Tracey Green, producer of the syndicated television show *Extra,* said the Speechworks Formula makes it as easy as 1-2-3.

RECAP

I. Tell 'em what's in it for them: MO
1.
2.
3.

II. Tell 'em
1. Illustrate
2. Illustrate
3. Illustrate

III. Tell 'em what you just told 'em: Recap MO
1.
2.
3.

1-2-3, 1-2-3, 1-2-3. Waltz your way to success!

4

Good Visuals,
Like Cologne,
Linger Longer
with the Listener

When you're wooing hearts, minds, and contracts, show up with something that excites the eye and makes your presentation memorable. Simple pictures, icons, or cartoons, like flowers, get noticed. These attention grabbers show that you cared enough to bring your very best support.

Great visuals make a big difference. Audiences remember 80 percent of what they see and only 20 percent of what they hear. A picture supported by text keeps an audience awake, on track, and reinforces your message whether you use slides, video, computer-generated graphics, overheads, flip charts, boards, or props.

Text slides or overheads, on the other hand, can dull the interest of even the most eager prospect. We worked on the fund-raising presentation for a major metropolitan hospital. Fifty-three of their slides were text. Only three slides showed doctors and patients together. The presentation was painful. The hospital's patients lived, but the presentation died.

> " A picture is worth a thousand words. "
>
> —A Chinese proverb

VISUALS WORK FOR YOUR LISTENERS

"Don't kill your listeners with Bullets."
—Speechworks

✔ They grab their attention.

✔ They increase retention.

Bullets Kill

Corporate America commits "death by overheads" daily. Audiences have visibly gone to their knees when a presenter flicks on the overhead switch to reveal a bulleted list. Shoulders sag, bodies go limp, and eyes glaze over. The audience is down for the count before the presenter says a word.

Don't be conned by the corporate tradition of using text slides to inform. It may be the standard for business communication, but it has more value as an anesthetic than as a communication tool. When was the last time you heard someone in a meeting say, "Good presentation, but it would have been better with more bullets!"

The Broadcast Media Is a Role Model

TV weatherfolks have learned how symbols or simple pictures can make meteorology memorable.

In Atlanta, WXIA-TV weatherman Guy Sharpe said, "Pictures help us tell the weather story without sounding like teachers. Simple pictures help us tell complicated information about fronts, storms, and changing weather patterns. We use the K.I.S.S. method [keep it simple, speaker] approach. Visuals also help us make weather information available to the hearing impaired."

The same techniques are emerging in business today. Pie charts and graphs are the visuals of choice in corporate America. Take a look at the emerging graphics trend in magazines including *Businessweek, U.S. News & World Report,* and *Fortune.* Newspapers such as *USA Today* use picture graphs that relate statistics to the subject and draw the eye to the data.

Color adds energy. *USA Today* led the way with color in a daily newspaper—and now even the *New York Times* has it.

Visuals Simplify Concepts

Visuals make information easy to grasp. Overheads with words may help a speaker organize and deliver the message, but to the listener's eye, text on the screen becomes just a blurred, gray pattern, with no take-away value. When words appear, most of us bounce back and forth from reading to listening and lose information with each shift.

The mind thinks and stores information visually. Maps, blueprints, machine diagrams, logos, dollar signs, stock market arrows, and even dreams, are part of our visual memories. The right symbol brings the idea to life and tells the story. If you cannot picture your concept, you have not thought it out. Make it simple to make the listener feel smart.

Pictures Have Staying Power

Audiences may forget a speaker's words 30 minutes after a presentation, but they can take a test on the pictures a week later. Play the popular game Pictionary and brainstorm picture ideas that convey your information. In the game, you must convey your ideas in a picture. In the game of *Charades,* the quicker the team gets the message, the greater the score. Try these examples:

Use grocery bags, instead of a bar graph, to compare highs and lows in food sales over a five-year period.

Put a large building next to a smaller one to show which construction company has the greater sales.

Chart ups and downs of a cruise line's operations as the course of a ship's cruise.

Choose a clock, a coin, or a cross-cut of a log to make an effective pie chart.

Picture a dollar bill being passed from hand to hand to represent the term *cash flow*.

Draw an exit sign to reinforce the word *downsizing* in a presentation.

Use a photograph of a forest as the background visual for a presentation on the environment.

Example of using meaningful pictures to convey an idea.

Illustrative Props Build Relationships

Renee Levow, a specialist in 401K plans and a vice president at the Robinson Humphrey Company built a rapport with her seminar audience with props.

She opened the workshop with the comment, "Let's cut through the red tape," as she swept the air with Darth Vader's sword from her child's toy box. "It was risky business using the props," she commented. "But I found my seminar participants were much more responsive on a personal level when I made follow-up calls. The props humanized me as a financial expert. I was surprised at how much they remembered about the information I covered. Their willingness to talk gave me insights into their financial picture and resulted in new business."

Props are big business. Trial lawyers buy anatomical props to explain victims' complicated injuries to juries. They build scale models to simulate accidents.

Demonstrations Engage

A product demonstration live or on video, a simple series of slides, even a drawing on a paper napkin will help you demonstrate your idea.

Ad man Joey Reiman, chairman of Bright House and author of *The Handbook* (Longstreet Press), gave a talk to a group of entrepreneurs about what it takes to succeed in business. He offered five points each illustrated by a different finger on his hand.

He began with a thumbs up gesture to signal a positive attitude. Then he said, "Use your index finger to point at what you want. Be determined and give the middle finger gesture to fear. Use the fourth finger to remember to march forth toward your goal. The little finger is your reminder of the importance of little things, like a smile, a thank you and a phone call." A simple message, creatively illustrated and instantly remembered.

The importance of maintaining your investment.

VISUALS WORK FOR YOU

✔ *Visuals clarify your ideas.* Create a visual for your big ideas. Pictures help clarify the point or concept you want to convey. Ask yourself, "What is the point of each visual and what message will the listener get?" As each question is answered you will be able to simplify or correct the visual.

✔ *Visuals keep you on track.* They give you a personal road map. When each main point has an icon, you know where you are in your presentation.

✔ *Visuals break down language barriers.* Imagine listening to an entire presentation in German supported with bulleted text in German. Simple pictures build relationships and increase comfort.

Greg Gregory, president and CEO of IDI, Industrial Developments International greeted his Japanese colleagues in Japanese. His presentation was in English. Although they UNDERSTOOD English, the visuals "brought the complex new concept home."

✔ *Visuals add interest.* An executive giving an update on the international product expansion of his organization interspersed the bullets with pictures of famous locations in each country. It reduced the text and allowed him to conversationally relate the statistics to the setting.

✔ *Visuals build confidence.* Visuals are your partner in a strong, memorable presentation. If you use written notes, consider a visual storyboard that will give you cues to talk about rather than *read* about (see page 60).

ADD POW TO YOUR PRESENTATION

✔ Preparation

✔ Originality

✔ Workable materials

Sit in the chair of the listener. Would you prefer a 60-slide information dump from which you try to obtain a few concepts? Or would you like a snapshot of what the information will do for you, targeted to your eyes and ears? Give 'em concepts and conclusions and provide backup data in a handout.

Preparation

Translate your information into pictures. Create quick-read visuals that instantly reinforce your message and stick like glue in the mind of the listener. Visuals will reduce the time spent in meetings by 28 percent according to a study at the Wharton Center for Applied Research.

Take the key concept of your Message Objective and three points and visualize them. For example, in our Quick Fix example (see chapter 1), our MO was, "*Wooing & Winning Business* will build business for you and your company."

Your Hook, MO, and three points are your concept visuals. You can add to these five concept visuals, depending on the length of the presentation. Plan for no more than one visual per minute.

The three points were:

1. Build your case persuasively by using the Speechworks Formula.

2.

2. Present it with confidence.

3. Use the Formula to win in all types of business presentations.

3.

Charts and Graphs

Without a visual connection to the subject, all graphs look alike . . . only their creator recognizes them. Statistics as illustrations of your points need not be flat, threatening, and anonymous. They can tell your story in a picture. See the following samples for ideas.

1. *Fever Chart.*   Quantities plotted over a time period; a fast look at the flow of a set of figures

2. *Bar Chart.*   Visualization of quantities; used to show comparison of different commodities

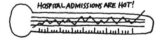

3. *Pie Chart.*   Division of whole into parts, usually in percentages

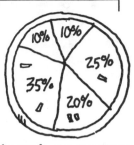

LUIGI'S - A SLICE ABOVE

Create a Storyboard

Storyboards are used by ad agencies, movie makers, and superb business presenters like you to plot the path of presentations.

Storyboards will help make the biggest impact on your audience. They also serve as a visual script that will prompt you through your presentation. With practice, you will find it easier and more persuasive to talk about your visuals than to read a written script.

Here is a sample storyboard. Begin with a title slide. Put it up before the presentation begins. If it is for a new or important business presentation, create a visual that includes your prospect's as well as your own logo. Otherwise, use a cover slide that includes your logo.

A content storyboard without logos.

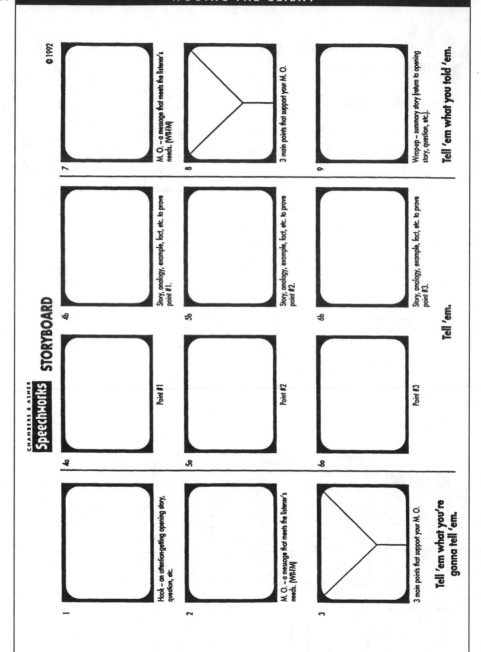

CHAMBERS & ASHER
Speechworks STORYBOARD

1 — Hook — an attention-getting opening story, question, etc.

2 — M. O. — a message that meets the listener's needs. (WIIFM)

3 — 3 main points that support your M. O.

Tell 'em what you're gonna tell 'em.

4a — Point #1
5a — Point #2
6a — Point #3

4b — Story, analogy, example, fact, etc. to prove point #1.
5b — Story, analogy, example, fact, etc. to prove point #2.
6b — Story, analogy, example, fact, etc. to prove point #3.

Tell 'em.

7 — M. O. — a message that meets the listener's needs. (WIIFM)

8 — 3 main points that support your M. O.

9 — Wrap-up — summary story (return to opening story, question, etc.).

Tell 'em what you told 'em.

Originality

Cartoons, clip art, computer clip art, photos, and icons can tell your story. *Dover Handbook of Pictorial Symbols* (from Dover Publications, New York) is a source of out-of-copyright illustrations that can be copied, colored, or enlarged.

LAUNCH

TEAMWORK

HIGH TECH

An amateur artist in your office, a student, or a professional can be enlisted to create cartoon visuals. Sara Dyck, manager of Consulting Services at Smith Barney, uses simple hand-drawn overheads to introduce brokers to a complex area of investing. A senior broker, having seen and heard her presentation said, "That's the first time I've ever truly understood the opportunities that TRAX offers my clients."

COMMUNICATE

Create Consistent Well-Dressed Computer Graphics

Beware: Computer literacy does not indicate a good sense of design and balance when creating slides.

✔ Use a program, such as PowerPoint, that offers background templates to give a consistent color scheme and design.

✔ Choose no more than three letter styles (fonts) for a slide or overhead presentation.

✔ Color adds impact—limit your color palate to three main colors. Use others as accents to highlight key words or add spice to your visuals. Dark backgrounds hide the inevitable dust that projects like snakes on the screen.

✔ Add your company logo to the corner of every visual.

✔ Include the prospective client's logo in a new business presentation.

✔ Reference the point being made with a symbol in a corner of the visual if you have several visuals concerning one point.

✔ Choose uniform clip art. Don't mix and match styles. Just as you wouldn't wear a pinstriped jacket with plaid slacks, you should avoid mixing icons and cartoons in most cases.

Workable Materials

Choose your weapons. With all electronic media, have a backup in case of equipment failure.

PRACTICE, PRACTICE, PRACTICE

"Details, details, details," shouted Alvin Flanagan, former chairman of Gannett Broadcasting. An error-free TV show or a great presentation is in the details. Practice with your visuals to look like a pro. Here are tips that will help you create a seamless presentation.

✔ Know the room in advance. If possible, the screen should be to the side. You should be at the center.

✔ Face the listener, not the visuals. Keep your toes forward to force you to look forward. Talk to your listener, *never to the visual.*

MEDIA OPTIONS FOR VISUALS

	Flipcharts	Boards and Props	Overheads	Computer	Slides	Video Tape
Audience size	Under 20 people.	Under 20 people.	About 100 people.	Depends on size of screen.	Several hundred people.	Small or large.
Design complexity	Simple. Can be done during program.	Hand done or Computer-generated blowups.	Simple. Can be made on office copier.	Needs computer skill.	Anything that can be photo-graphed.	Anything that can be shot with a video camera.
Equipment and room require-ments	Easel and paper.	Visuals mounted on foam core boards.	Projector and screen.	Computer monitor alone or with LCD projector, panel, and screen.	Projector and screen.	Video monitor, large screen or multiple monitors.
Production time	Drawing time.	Blow up and copy time.	Drawing or typing time; may be copied instantly.	Varies. Can be changed on site.	Design and photo-graphing time plus at least 24 hours pro-duction time.	Varies. From simple testimonials to edited multilocation video tape.
Cost	Inexpen-sive unless profes-sionally drawn.	The price is reasonable.	Home-made cost-free to costly.	Use of existing software.	From $20 each and up.	Homemade to costly.
Consider-ations	Use to record listener feedback.	A copier store such as Kinko can blow up or mount boards in black and white or color.	• Present with lights on and maintain good eye contact. • Be inter-active and record lis-tener feed-back on an overhead.	• Viewer may be more inter-ested in computer tricks than in your in-formation. • Needs support operator.	• A dark room will kill your relationship with listeners. • Darken front of room; keep lights on in back.	Keep it short. No more than three to five minutes.

✔ Place a green dot (indicator) on the forward button of your slide changer to avoid mishaps.

✔ Wait for the visual to appear before speaking.

✔ Gesture toward the visual with the arm closest to it.

✔ Preview the information on a word/number visual verbally before going into detail on your information. As a result the listener is not distracted by reading ahead. This is called taking the news value off the visual.

✔ Don't overpower a small group with a slide or overhead that is over-sized.

✔ Prepare to "fly solo." Visuals are a great partner, but if they desert you, the show must go on.

✔ "Visuals are a great prop, but they aren't the show," says attorney Gardner Courson, senior partner of Glass, McCullough, Sherill & Harrold. "I followed a speaker with the most beautiful slides that you have ever seen, but it didn't matter because he was the most boring speaker." And that's the truth.

Simple visuals are a universal language that help you to amuse, engage, and connect with your listener. Successful wooers know that you can't bore anybody into buying anything, but savvy speakers can enhance a presentation with visuals as a partner.

RECAP

MO: Visuals keep the listener tuned in.

→ Reinforce your message with visuals.

→ Increase retention by over 50 percent.

→ Practice with visuals to avoid distractions and to look smoother.

5

Inquiring Minds Want to Know: Handling Questions and Answers

When the listener pops the questions and your heart begins to race, relax. Questions in one-on-one meetings, small team presentations, or large sales seminars are the business speaker's winning opportunity. They let you know immediately what's on your listeners' mind, how they feel about your message.

Inquiring minds want to know. Buyers and boards ask the darndest questions. The minute they do pop a question, your job is to answer positively, turn objections into opportunity, and control your destiny.

A tough-sounding question can work to your advantage. The worse it sounds, the more others tune in. A well-thought-out answer will get the audience's attention and allow you to score points that add to your credibility.

> **"** Does anyone have any questions for the answers that I have prepared? **"**
> —Henry Kissinger

PLAN AHEAD

Hard Questions Made Easy

Most people strategize their presentations and wing the Q&A. Not a good idea. Most people don't

plan the Q&A because they believe the questions are unpredictable. Not true. If you know your audience and their hot buttons, you can predict eight out of ten questions. President Bush and his communication team had an 85 percent accuracy rate in predetermining the questions the media would ask during press conferences. You can do the same. Brainstorm the very worst questions in advance. Prepare good, solid responses to each. Keep it brief. Prepare to make a point and illustrate it.

The *murder board* is the military term for a Q&A practice session. Have your peers hurl the softball and hardball questions at you. And then *practice.* Recruit outsiders to lob questions at you—outsiders who may have the same concerns as your audience. Team members are often so close to the situation that they come up with overly complex questions and fail to prepare for the simple ones. Ask outsiders for questions they would ask. Consider cultural differences that would change the attitude of your questioners. What questions would a CEO ask? What are the objections you can expect from the human resources department or the CFO.

Record the Rehearsal

Record the Q&A rehearsal on tape. The feedback from peers and your own personal assessment will improve your performance. A good rehearsal of basic and combative questions in the comfort of your own office builds confidence and eliminates a blind-side attack by decision makers.

Observe your presence as you answer questions. Are you open? (You should be.) Closed? (This is a mistake—your audience will think you are hiding something.) Is your hand over your mouth? (It shouldn't be.) Do you nod as you listen? (If the question is negative, you may seem to agree.)

Watch the Signals

Some questions trigger reactions that tend to make your team members feel combative and defensive. Questions work like traffic lights: red signals hostile or aggressive; yellow flashes warning; green gives the go ahead for a cool, informational answer. Your responses should always be green.

Although you can't walk in questioners' well-worn shoes, you can sense that they have mileage and baggage that makes them ask the yellow or red light questions. Before you respond, flash on your own yellow caution light and ask yourself, "Why this question?" You'll gain a new perspective and be able to clearly, patiently explain your position.

General Norman Schwarzkopf was the coach in his briefings and press conferences during Operation Desert Storm. He did not aggressively defend his actions. He patiently explained the strategy and how they came to each decision to act. That is the green light approach.

Eliminate the Negative

If you have ever watched a courtroom drama on TV, you know that there are two sides to every situation. In answering questions, make sure that your side is told clearly, confidently, and backed up with evidence.

If the question has a negative slant such as, "Why are your fees so high?" it is your job to change the perspective. Repeat the question in a positive way, "Let me explain our fee structure."

Reagan did it well in answering questions on the Equal Rights Amendment (ERA). After raising the ire of his listeners when asked his attitude on the subject, he gave a positive answer. "I believe in equal rights for women, but I think there are other means to handle the situation." You may not have agreed with him, but his positive response kept you tuned in.

Take a Team Approach to Answering Questions

Guy Patton, president of Patton Construction Company in Atlanta, said that he and his team had anticipated the major questions that would be asked in a recent hospital presentation. "When the question was asked about the company's experience on a certain project, each of our team members answered in a specific, personal way based on their area of expertise. The cumulative responses, rather than one answer, achieved broader credibility."

Add the Human Touch

Honesty and caring builds trust in a Q&A session. So does the ability to show your human side.

A corporate crisis can be anything from the Dow Corning breast implant suit or the Exxon *Valdez* oil spill to keeping an unhappy client with you after a debacle. The key to damage control is listening and caring. Even the ever wary lawyers we work with say that showing concern is acceptable and won't interfere with a lawsuit. Exxon stonewalled the public. The chairman's failure to go to the scene of the accident and show concern for the environment increased the wrath of the public and their stockholders. Listen, and listen with concern. Even if you can't fix the situation, show respect for those involved.

CONTROL THE MECHANICS OF Q&A IN A LARGE GROUP SETTING

Question and answer sessions in one-to-one meetings or team presentations are smaller and more focused than in sales seminars. Larger audiences present a wider range of potential questions.

Jump-Start the Q&A Session

Questions in a seminar are often slow to start. People need time to think. They fear the reactions of the speaker or they just don't want to go first. To start the ball rolling, say, "The question I'm most asked is, 'How do we gauge the risk of this strategy?' or 'Before the program, Jim asked. . . .'" It is also acceptable to plant a question in the audience.

When the questions do begin to roll, reward the questioners. Thank them for asking. Avoid saying, "That's a good question." Others may think theirs weren't.

Three Reasons There Are No Questions

1. You talked too long and they want lunch.
2. You offended someone and they are punishing you.
3. They don't understand and are afraid to ask a dumb question.

Repeat the Question

Keep listeners involved and interested by repeating a question. This allows the listener in the back of the room who initially didn't hear the question to stay involved. It also slows down the momentum, gives you time to think, and helps you take control if the situation is hostile.

Control a Multifaceted Question

When a member of the audience asks, "What are your plans for the new 'X' product? Why is it costing so much? When will it be introduced?" Smile and take the opportunity to unbundle the question. Answer, "You have asked me three questions. Let me answer them one at a time." Then you choose which question you will answer first.

A doctor we worked with answered a multifaceted medical question by saying, "Let me answer the second question first, and then I'll move on to one and three if we have time." Control the situation and your destiny.

If You Don't Know an Answer, Ask for Help

In a Q&A situation, you are not the only expert in the room. If you get a zinger you can't handle, ask a colleague or get input from the group. There is a wealth of experiences in the room. You will be rewarded with a world of new ideas on the subject. This is a great opportunity to interact—to show leadership.

If you are alone and clueless about the answer to a question, don't panic. Admit it. Build trust by promising to get the answer and get back to the questioner quickly. Good communication skills are not about perfection, but connection.

Avoid Embarrassing an Attendee

If an attendee repeats a previously asked question, answer it again in a different way or with a different example. This is your opportunity to show that you are a class act. Listeners will side with the questioner if you are rude, thinking, "That could have been me."

Handling a Statement Dressed Up Like a Question

Competitors may attend your seminar. They can ask needling questions or leap up to make long-winded statements.

Take a tip from CNN's Larry King. He is quick to interrupt ramblers with, "What is your question?" Seminar audiences are on your side and don't want their time taken over by a speaker in search of an audience.

If one listener is needling you, ask for the attendee's name and company. This can quickly show up competitors or calm down a protagonist.

Avoid the Over-Heated Discussion or Fight

Listeners look to you to take control of a hot room or a hot temper. Take charge quickly and don't let a difficult situation go unchecked.

If two people get over-heated about a point, step in between and say, "You seem excited about this point. I'd like to know both sides." Look at one and ask, "How do you feel about the situation?" Then ask the other, "What's your side?"

Get the problem out in the open. Keep your remarks balanced. Giving each participant air time often resolves the situation. If the situation continues to be heated, ask them to join you afterward and then take others' questions.

THE BODY LANGUAGE OF A LEADER

Presence is critical for maintaining control in any size Q&A. Check your body language when you answer questions. This is the time to look and act like a leader. Come out from behind the podium or stand beside the table. Eliminate barriers between you and your listener.

Stand or sit with authority, lean forward, hands open, not clasped. Make eye contact with the questioner, then move on and share your answer with others. Many listeners may have the same question.

This is also a good method of controlling the *dominator,* the one who likes to talk. Look at the person as the question is asked, then move on and look at someone else as you answer. As you finish your answer, move your gaze and your body to another part of the room.

Show interest in the questioner's concern, even if the questions make you prickly. Dump folded arms or pointed fingers. Forget the bobbing head reaction. It can telegraph anything from "I agree," when you don't, to "hurry up and finish." Stay cool and resist the temptation to interrupt. Your body action speaks louder than words.

END WITH RECAPPING

End the Q&A with impact. Insure that decision makers leave with your Message Objective and three points firmly in hand. Close a one-to-one or group meeting, a team presentation, or a large seminar with a final recap of your MO and three points followed by a call to action. In that way you control the final message that the listener takes away.

RECAP

MO: Questions are an opportunity to build credibility.

→ Plan ahead for Q&A by predetermining the tough and easy questions.

→ Answer patiently, not defensively.

→ Act and look like a leader.

PART 2

ALL THE RIGHT MOVES

> She had all the right moves. Her hands moved with
> ease, in confident control. Her voice was slow and
> deliberate and then raced ahead with excitement.
> The experience took her to new heights.

LET'S GET PHYSICAL: THE 93 PERCENT SOLUTION

Dr. Albert Mehrabian, a UCLA communications researcher, says that the visual you—posture, gestures, and movement—accounts for 55 percent of what the audience believes, the impression you make. Voice energy accounts for 38 percent of the impression you make. That is the 93 percent solution. Without it, the listener will tune out your information . . . the 7 percent.

This section shows how to connect with your listener using the five basic skills of delivery: stance, eye contact, gestures, movement, the 55 percent; and voice energy and the pause, the 38 percent. You will learn how your stance and the way you sit can convey the message that you are open and confident, even if you don't feel that way. When you court a customer it is not *what* you say, but *the way* that you say it that wins hearts and handshakes. You will learn how to strengthen a male or female voice and develop the power of the pause.

There are simple techniques in this book that will give you the confidence to sound like you mean it, the courage to speak with passion.

You've been using these skills since you were 18 months old. Knowing the right body language jump-starts your confidence and assures you that even if you don't feel like a pro, you look like a winner.

Before you start learning these skills, there's one obstacle you may have to overcome. Most people say that speaking to a group makes them nervous. Public speaking is cited as the number one fear, ahead of health problems. Performance anxiety is normal. As TV producers, we saw this with many *Noonday* guests just before they went on the set. The pros know how to deal with it. They expect it. Chapter 6 shows you how to dodge nervous splotches and defeat that internal, yipping, self-defeating voice. It shows you how to cope with the heart-thumping, knee-knocking nerves your body comes up with when you make that important presentation.

Rehearsing is the energizer. It eliminates fumbling and faltering. Each *rehearing* builds familiarity with the content, jump-starts the delivery, and plants giant seeds of confidence. In Chapter 14, you'll learn how to avoid rehearsal hell and practice on camera.

No excuses. You communicate every day in this changing work environment. You can't afford not to be your best to ensure career success.

SIX MOST COMMON EXCUSES
FOR GIVING BORING PRESENTATIONS

1. **"I'm the strong, silent type."**
   Did you get excited when you sunk a winning putt or saw your children walk for the first time? Did you reach out and cheer them on? With voice energy you will sound like you believe in your subject.

2. **"It's not part of our culture; people don't do things that way around here."**
   Translation: Our president is a bore. It's peer pressure. The leader of an organization sets the tone and it can become an excuse for taking the safe, stiff route. Until you become the chief and your staff has to listen because of who you are, you will have to depend on your content and your delivery to hold your listeners' attention.

3. **"I'm not an actor."**
   Oh, no? Well, do you wear that business suit/costume on Saturday? What do you do when a person greets you with "Hi Randy, how's it going?" and you haven't a clue who it is?. . . . That's acting.

4. **"My information speaks for itself."**
   What is *heard* depends on *how you speak.* You have to keep them awake if you want them to hear it.

5. **"I'm so nervous. I'll just read it and keep it short."**
   A conversational communicator seems less nervous than a motionless monotone.

6. **"The audience has already made up its mind."**
   A well-documented, convincingly presented case will add to your credibility. You may not get the win, but you will make a positive impression that builds your long-term reputation. A construction client we worked with did lose the business presentation, but its presentation was so impressive that they were called to make a proposal shortly after that loss. The next round, they won.

6
Never Let 'Em See You Sweat

Everyone from trembling amateurs to seasoned veterans experiences performance anxiety. If this describes you just moments before giving a business presentation you are not alone.

In his book, *You Are the Message,* Roger Ailes, chairman of CNBC and former producer of the *Merv Griffin Show,* described his dealings with a Marine Corps general, a heroic Vietnam veteran and Medal of Honor recipient. Five minutes before airtime the general said to Ailes, "I'm not going on the show."

In desperation, Ailes challenged him. "Either you're going to walk out and talk, or I'm going out in place of you and tell everybody you're chicken." Ailes' challenge put the general's fears in perspective. The general went on and did well. Courage is not the absence of fear. It is action in the presence of fear.

"Being aware that nervousness is normal is a key to dealing with the anxiety of making a presentation," says Steven Garber, psychologist with the Behavioral Institute of Atlanta. "The beginning of controlling nerves is confronting the fears and

> "According to most studies, people's number one fear is public speaking. Number two is death. Death is number two. Does that seem right? That means to the average person, if you have to go to a funeral, you're better off in the casket than doing the eulogy."
>
> —Jerry Seinfeld, from *SeinLanguage*

their manifestations and then dealing with them.” Garber's clients usually come to him because they have come to a career crossroads. They know that being unable to give a presentation successfully means not moving ahead in their career. They are petrified to stand in front of a group . . . of any size.

Treatment begins by looking back to determine the root of the fear and then confronting it in its worst manifestations. For example, Garber had a client whose mouth became so dry, he was afraid he wouldn't be able to speak. Garber had him eat saltine crackers, then speak, proving to himself that he indeed could speak, even with a dry mouth.

EXPECT TO BE NERVOUS

Even the pros get nervous. Anticipation seems to be worse than action. Until golfers get off the first tee, they feel nervous. Athletes prepare to take the field, actors stand in the wings, and physiological nervousness takes over. In our workshops the great epiphany happens when our terrified clients see their first videotape and see that even if they are terrified, the nervousness doesn't show. And if it doesn't show, no one can see it—you can live with it.

NO WHINING

Never let 'em see you sweat, or hear you say it either. Don't announce: “I'm so nervous.” Or “I'm not a speaker.” These comments diminish you and your message. Most of all, it makes the audience very uncomfortable. “A speaker's nerves are the most communicable disease in the world," said the late attorney and author, Louis Nizer.

TURN PRESENTATION PANIC INTO PRESENTATION POWER USING THE THREE Ps: PREPARATION, PHYSICAL FITNESS, AND A POSITIVE MENTAL ATTITUDE

"Off the cuff is off the mark."
—Speechworks

Preparation

1. *Know your information.* Fifty percent of nervousness can be controlled by preparation. Know your subject and believe in it. Off the cuff is off the mark. Use the Chambers and Asher Speechworks Formula. Instead of worrying about making a mistake, sharpen your organization and practice.

2. *Know your opening and closing cold.* Memorize it. A confident start will get you going. Find a short, punchy opening grabber that you can say easily with conviction even when your heart is pounding. (See chapter 3.) Prepare a closing. That way you won't feel the panic of "how am I going to get out of this thing?" It is important to end . . . not just ramble on and then drift away!

3. *Plan ahead to answer questions.* Think of the common objections and questions that will come along. Determine the five worst questions you could be asked. Plan well-thought-out answers. (See chapter 5.)

4. *Practice.* Rehearse your material two or three times before your presentation. The story is

"Courage is doing what you are afraid to do. There is no courage unless you are scared."

—Unknown

told that shipping magnate, Aristotle Onassis, was often seen pacing the deck of his yacht at dawn. Once, a steward, alarmed to see him, asked if there was a problem. Onassis replied, "No. I have an important meeting this morning and I'm practicing my presentation."

5. *Arrive early.* Check out the room and make it familiar. Check equipment so you are confident it will work. Introduce yourself to people as they arrive so you'll feel connected with members of the audience from the beginning. These people will be your security blanket. During your presentation you can make eye contact and look to them for feedback.

6. *Volunteer to speak.* Force yourself to accept the challenge. Teach a Sunday school class. Seek a leadership role in a volunteer organization. This will give you a familiarity with standing before a group and prepare you to be more comfortable in front of a business group.

Positive Mental Attitude

1. *Think positively.* In the musical *How to Succeed in Business Without Really Trying,* the young hero looks into the mirror and sings, "You've got the cool, clear eyes of a seeker of wisdom and truth. . . . I believe in you, I believe in you."

2. *Talk to yourself in a positive way.* From the time you get the call to make a business presentation up to the time you stand before the group, tell yourself, "I have information that will make my audience richer, smarter, healthier, and happier," rather than, "I hate to speak, this is going to be terrible."

3. *Enjoy the ridiculous.* Often the fear is not the *how many* but the *who* we must address. If that is the case, take a tip attributed to Winston Churchill. As prime minister, he humanized the British parliament by picturing them sitting on the john!

4. *Be audience-centered.* Instead of being self-centered, think of yourself as a problem solver and a coach. Fear is rooted in, "What will they think of me?" The solution is to think of what you can do for them.

After we wrote *TV PR, How to Promote Yourself, Your Product, Your Service or Your Organization on Television,* Spring was invited to appear on CNN. She commented to the host that she was nervous. He left her in the studio with her doubts and fears about *her* performance. The host returned ten minutes later and said, "Get over it . . . don't ruin my show!" It was the right message: Be listener-centered, not self-centered.

Get Physical

1. *Exercise.* It reduces the tension that heightens panic. It gets your blood flowing and energy level up. Athletes, like communicators, are nervous before a competition. They establish a systematic prepresentation warm-up routine. You should, too. Do neck rolls on the way to the presentation. Include a mirror check, an aerobic and anaerobic exercise.

Exercise before a presentation. Take a long walk in the parking lot or work out at home. Comedian Billy Crystal does 150 push-ups before going out on stage. He says, "I like to break a sweat."

Warm up your voice by having a prepresentation conversation with group members. Laugh and enjoy in order to relax.

2. *Establish a calming routine.* Do isometric exercises while you are waiting to speak. No one will notice. Tense and release muscles four or five times and the muscles will begin to relax. For example, make a fist and release it.

Try the Valsalva maneuver: Sit tall, put your feet on the floor, clasp your hands, press your palms together, and push down (as if you were constipated)—count to six and release. This cuts off the adrenaline flow and physiologically reduces nervousness.

3. *Breathe from the diaphragm.* Shallow breathing from the chest causes shortness of breath and a high-pitched voice. Try this exercise that gives you the same lazy, comfortable breathing that you use as you wake up in the morning: Inhale for four counts (stomach goes out), hold for two, and exhale for six (stomach goes in).

4. *Make eye contact as you speak.* Focus on one set of eyes as you begin. Then move through the group. This technique simulates the one-on-one conversations we are most comfortable with and shuts out visual distractions. (See the section on eye contact in chapter 8.)

5. *Fake it til you make it!* "Whenever I feel afraid I hold my head erect—and whistle a happy tune—and no one will suspect I'm afraid," were the words Anna sang in *The King and I.* ". . . The result of this deception—is very plain to tell—for when I fool the people I fear, I fool myself as well."

Perception is reality. Act as if you are confident, and you will come across that way.

RECAP

MO: Nervous 'is Normal.' You learned:

→ Preparation reduces tension.

→ A positive mental attitude increases confidence.

→ Physical activity reduces stress.

7
Confidence Is Sexy: Presence

"**C**onfidence is so very sexy," says actor Jack Palance in his Mennen Aftershave commercials. You communicate confidence with your body. Listeners can't see your credentials, but they can see how you stand, feel your energy, and experience your eye contact. Put on your boots and spurs and stand proud and tall. A good stance is like a firm handshake—it indicates a can-do attitude.

Take a look at actors Charles Bronson, Rhea Perlman (from *Cheers*), and Anthony Hopkins. It is their presence, not their appearance, that is commanding. We are attracted to people who appear to have a sense of self.

Hugh McColl, the driving force behind the growth of NationsBank, is only five feet tall. He has been described by one business associate as "the only person I know who can strut sitting down." If Hugh can do it, so can you.

DO A PRESENCE MAKEOVER

✔ *Stand up.* Put your feet about a foot apart, with your toes forward and one foot slightly ahead of the other.

✔ *Center yourself on the balls of your feet, not back on your heels.*
Golf, basketball, tennis, and baseball players are on the balls of their
feet when they are ready to play.

✔ *Don't lock your knees.* It can cut off your circulation. You could faint!

✔ *Relax your arms by your side, hands loose.*

✔ *Take a deep breath through your nose.* This will lift your chest and
align your body from head to toe. Relax your shoulders.

Now look in the mirror. You are looking good. Relaxed and confident.
When you stand like this you show that you are open and in control of
yourself and your information. Just as a golfer stands to address the ball,
in a starting position, you take your place before a presentation. By standing on the balls of your feet, your body is tipped slightly forward; toward
the goal, your listener!

Compare the neutral position to the following more defensive posi-
tions:

TAKING THE FLOOR

✔ Walk to the front of the room with energy, as though you can't wait to begin your presentation.

✔ Head up.

✔ Face forward and center yourself, balanced on both feet.

✔ Pause to get the listeners' attention. Take a breath.

✔ Make eye contact with one individual to get comfortable. Smile.

✔ Count to five. Let them wait. Now speak.

LEAVING THE STAGE

✔ Pause (for the applause) before leaving to sit down.

✔ Don't rush to leave.

The pause at the beginning and end is a sign of confidence.

WHAT TO DO WHEN YOU'RE SITTING DOWN

Study the TV anchors who sit to present twenty-four hours a day.

✔ Sit up, butt up against the back of the chair.

✔ Lift your chest. Lean in toward the speaker.

✔ If there is a table put your hands on the table. They should be open, not clasped. Take up some space, it adds to your presence.

✔ If there is no table, open your arms on the arms of the chair or on your thighs, not closed in your lap.

The importance of presence was brought home to us when a young accountant at a Big Six firm, a rising manager, came into a workshop, in a wheelchair. She looked frail; her arms were in her lap. Her shoulders slouched forward. We asked her to lift her chest, to put her arms on the wheels of the chair (it had no arm rests).

The difference was amazing. She saw herself and the change in her image on-camera. She said, "This program was more valuable to me than any client you will have." She was not the frail person she appeared to be that first morning. Just by changing her carriage, she came across as the strong, confident Elite Paralympic wheelchair athlete that she is.

TO STAND OR SIT, THAT IS THE QUESTION

Always stand to present during a group presentation, if there is a choice. It honors those who've come to listen. It shows presence, control, and adds to your voice energy.

Look for an opportunity to stand during a seated meeting. Stand to use a flip chart. Stand to pass out and discuss a handout.

Sergio Cruz, consultant at Kurt Salmon Associates, knows it works. "I was in a meeting with the

Chairman of a large clothing manufacturer. He had a very dominating personality. I was warned that he could get up and walk out of a meeting.

"I could see things beginning to go badly. I stood, to make my point, the Chairman listened. By standing, I took control and looked more confident as I discussed changes that would return the company to profitability. As a result the changes were made."

RECAP

MO: A confident presence commands attention.

→ Put on your boots and spurs to show presence.

→ Project an open presence—hands at your sides when not in use.

→ Walk with determination.

8
Let's Face It: Eye Contact and Face Energy

THE EYES HAVE IT

What is it about eye contact that let's you know in a flash if there is trust? Why is it that you get this creepy feeling when you don't get eye contact?

Physically, eye contact builds trust. When you look a prospect in the eye, they feel important and involved. To get the business, you have to get the trust.

What impression does a listener get if you read or stare at the floor when you want to get your message across? If you can't make eye contact when making a presentation, send a memo!

Try this experiment with a friend. The next time she speaks to you, don't look at her. Then ask for her reactions to your lack of eye contact. Ask her how she felt about you, how she felt about what you were saying.

TV anchors make incredible electronic eye contact. Lesley Stahl, Tom Brokaw, Bernard Shaw, Diane Sawyer, Peter Jennings, Susan Rook, Dan Rather, and Katie Couric make viewers feel involved and important.

TV TelePrompters allow anchors to read news copy that rolls over the lens of the camera. They seem to make eye contact with you in your living room. You feel that each is looking right at you, relating to you, the listener.

ZERO IN ON ONE SET OF EYES

NBC anchor Bryant Gumbel says that he doesn't feel nervous talking to two million people. "I am talking to one and looking right at him or her."

Most people are comfortable and confident talking one-on-one. You can replicate this same comfort level by focusing on one set of eyes at a time. *Make eye contact when speaking to a small group of people by delivering a whole thought to one person* (for about four to six seconds). Feel the connection, then move on to someone else just as you do with your lunch group. Talk to John about sports, shift to Mary to talk about weather, and go to Jennie to talk about the chicken salad. If you make listeners and friends feel important, it's amazing how much better attention you will get.

One of the participants in our Workshop was terrified when speaking to a group. "So many eyes looking at me made me lose it," she said. She was astounded to discover when she looked at one set of eyes at a time it made her calmer, more in control.

In a large group have miniconversations with an individual in the front of the room. Move in a *Z* around the room. Focus on the woman in red in the back left of the room and the whole group sitting around her will feel connected. Talk to the blond in the middle section. Continue to find one easy-to-look-at person in every section. Turn your shoulders toward the target group and your whole audience will soon feel connected.

AVOID COMMON EYE DISTURBANCES

Sprinkler Head Motion

The sprinkler head system of eye contact is a jerky eye motion intended to cover a room by squirting out a quick glance at one person, then twitching to the next patch, and finally swinging back to hit each listener once again.

Grazing Eye Sweep

When you sweep over the tops of the heads in an effort to take in the entire room, you are apt to get distracted by the waiter in the back of the room precariously juggling a load of dishes. It can cause you to lose your train of thought and give the impression that someone or something is more interesting than your listeners.

Don't Get Derailed by Inattentive, Scowling Listeners

Some listeners don't make eye contact with you. They take notes, slump, and doodle when they listen. It helps them to concentrate, but it wrecks your concentration.

Stick with user-friendly people. When you feel confident and brave, move toward the doodler. If it's a small group, ask scowlers a question by name. Change the energy in your voice to get their attention. Pause to cause them to look up.

Hold that eye contact. Look trustworthy. The nickname "Tricky Dick Nixon" was the result of the shifty, nervous eye contact made by the late president.

FACIAL EXPRESSION

Face it. . . . Speakers who stand rigid and grim-faced before decision makers aren't the least bit convincing when they say, "I'm happy to be here today." There may be, "Yes, yes," on their lips, but there's, "Oh! No!" in their body language.

A smile is a handshake with your face. Expressions add emphasis to your words and energy to your voice. When you're excited, your eyes open wide and your eyebrows go up. If you're disappointed, they may come down.

Facial expression shows the listener how you feel about your message. It makes you believable. President Jimmy Carter has great charisma with a live audience. Because he doesn't use his eyebrows, on television his face is devoid of expression. A microphone filters out some voice energy and his voice sounds bland.

Each of us has over 80 muscles in our face, capable of making over 7,000 facial expressions. Actor Jim Carrey, of "Batman" fame, probably has many more expressions which account for his incredible movie success. If we have all of these expressions, why do so many choose just one . . . the stone face, or the perma-grin? Take your face out of park.

Watch the lack of facial expression of an eyewitness on the TV news. Most bystanders are so terrified by the situation and the camera that they only move their lips. Their face is lifeless, zapped of emotion.

Male and Female Faces

Men and women have different facial problems. Men control their natural enthusiastic, intense, or fun-loving selves to put on their *this is serious—I am a grown-up* stone face for a business presentation.

A young bank loan officer explained why he became expressionless in a presentation. "I felt that if I acted really calm, no one could see that I was nervous." But having the courage to be his engaging and witty self, he won over his prospective clients quickly and has increased his business.

Women, on the other hand, tend to tilt their heads or bob them up and down while speaking. They smile to please. Heads up! Smile when you are pleased, not *to* please.

Try This Exercise

Lower your eyebrows and say, "I'm glad to be with you today." Now put your eyebrows at normal position and repeat the phrase. Finally, raise your eyebrows and say it: "I'm glad to be here today." Expressions increase energy.

Want a face-lift at no charge? Lift your cheeks as you listen and speak. You can look ten years younger!

RECAP

MO: Connect with your listener, one to one. It builds relationships.

→ Eye contact builds trust. You appear to believe in your subject.

→ Eye contact shows confidence. Have the courage to hold eye contact for a whole thought or idea.

→ A smile adds energy to your face and warmth to your presentation. Use the muscles in your face to add energy to the presentation.

9

Reach out and Touch Someone: Body Language

He shouted, "Yes!" stepped forward, and punched the air. Now that's a gesture. In an instant, you heard and felt the impact of his words. Gestures count when it comes to having all the right moves.

YES!

They add energy to your presentation and get rid of pent-up tension at the same time.

Umpires gesture best. When they reach forward, spread their arms, signal firmly, and shout, "Safe!" there is no doubt, no wimpy flailing about. The gesture is deliberate and quickly rules out doubt on the part of players or coaches.

The following ideas will add strength and conviction to your message.

AVOID STATIC CLING GESTURES

Speakers, not just pant liners, slips, and skirts experience static cling. Arms and hands get stuck to the middle or lower parts of your body and make you look nervous and defensive. Nothing flows or moves with ease. Hands get stuck in the fig leaf position. Fingertips cling to each other in the steeple at midchest. Elbows are stuck precariously at the waist, like a hinge.

A nervous, awkward cling is not a pretty sight.

You never see Arnold Schwarzenegger, Keanu Reeves, or Candice Bergen standing defensively with arms clinging to their body. They use their hands and arms to add energy and purpose. Their openness oozes confidence.

The following ideas will help you spray this problem away.

Let Your Armpits Breathe

Reach forward toward your listeners and hold the firm gesture. Reaching forward makes you look open and natural, the way you use your body when you talk to a buddy. Don't overthink gestures or movements. They should be a natural outgrowth of your conviction and energy.

Think Sports

All action in sports is forward, toward the goal: the hole in golf, the fence in baseball, the basket in basketball. Put your whole body into it—gesture toward a listener. Use the whole hand, no pointing. Hold it out there just as you hold the follow-through in sports.

ONE SMALL STEP

Astronaut Neil Armstrong took only three steps on the moon to make headlines. It can happen to you. Take a couple of steps. Movement releases tension, energizes your voice, and grabs the listeners' attention.

Walk firmly, don't pace. A pacer distracts a listener. Rocking distracts. Learning to move is like learning to dance. Take a couple of steps toward a listener at the right side of the room. Talk to an individual and another from that position, then move to the left. You can move while you talk or you can use the movement to breathe and regroup. The audience watches in anticipation. Walking is a perfect camouflage for nerves.

President Bill Clinton walks to the corner of the stage reaches forward and connects to an individual in the audience. His movement keeps the listeners focused. If you are going to move, be purposeful. The repetitive box step is boring. Do the tango . . . go somewhere.

If it's a really big show, use a lavalier mike and move. Podiums put a lock on movement. Movement behind a podium mike makes your voice fade in and out.

GET PHYSICAL

Describe your favorite room, physically. Have fun doing it and exaggerate for emphasis and to dis-

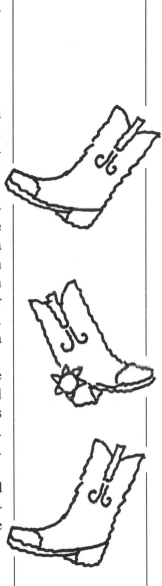

cover new gestures and movement that add impact. Set up your video camera so that you can sit in your audience and observe. See how good you look with firm gestures and you'll never wonder, "What do I do with my hands?" again.

✔ Make an extended arm gesture to show a picture window. Hold the gesture while you describe the view.

✔ Make a long, wide gesture with arms outstretched to describe your desk.

✔ Reach forward to show your Laz-E Boy recliner. Hold the gestures for a second or two to stamp out fast, jerky motions.

✔ Come back to the starting position—arms at your sides.

✔ Move from one side of the room to another to show other objects of interest.

✔ Gesture above the waist.

✔ Avoid *drawing* the square computer. Just indicate its placement on the desk.

Static cling gestures are awkward. Flailing gestures distract. Firm, deliberate gestures make you look more energized and make the audience feel that it is in good hands.

RECAP

MO: Gesture and move to energize your presentation.

→ Keep your listeners awake: Connect with them—move to them, reach out to them.

→ Gesture to add energy to your voice.

→ Move to reduce stress.

10
It's Not What You Say, but the Way That You Say It

"**I** vont to be alone," said Greta Garbo in her deep, sultry voice. Garbo was one of the few silent screen stars who made the transition to talkies in 1927. Others—even Rudolph Valentino—lost out because of their small, squeaky voices. They had little verbal presence.

Think of the commanding voices of actor James Earl Jones, General Norman Schwarzkopf, or poet Maya Angelou. Think of the conviction in the voice of Peter Finch who played Howard Beale in the movie "Network" when he said, "I'm mad as *hell,* and I'm *not* going to take it any more." It was not just the words, but the way he made you *feel* when he said them.

The voices of the characters George on *Seinfeld* or Melanie in *Gone With The Wind* are nervous and excitable. Similarly, a lack of confidence on the part of anyone pitching an idea or making a report creates doubt in even the most eager buyer.

Voice quality influences the way you are perceived. Speak with conviction and energy and your listener is tuned in. Drone on in a boring monotone and listeners take out their mental clicker and tune you out. With a simple change of pace you will see yourself transformed into the speaker that you want to be.

ADD SPICE TO YOUR PRESENTATION

Use voice variety. Take your listener on a verbal roller-coaster ride. Build excitement on the slow climb up the track to the top. Pause with anticipation. . . . Then a fast race down the incline (*pause . . .*) and begin the next soft ascent. This change of pace excites the listener more than a rambling train ride chugging from one stop to the next. . . . That's a sleeper.

Even those who say, "I'm talking numbers, and that's so boring," need to rethink voice energy. The bottom line is a top priority with business listeners. Your intensity, sincerity, and honesty need to come across in your voice.

CHANGE THE PACE

Loud, soft, slow, and *fast.* Read the following sentences as directed. You will be surprised at the incredible energy and interest you will be able to generate immediately. Read aloud daily to get your ear accustomed to a more dynamic voice. Try the sports pages and change the pace or volume from sentence to sentence. Read them into a tape recorder. Listen. Then try again.

Try This Exercise

Read the following sentences as directed.

Read *loudly:*
"VOLUME ADDS EMPHASIS TO AN IMPORTANT WORD OR PHRASE."

Read *softly:*
"A whisper acts as a magnet and pulls the listener to you."

Read *fast:*
"Speaking–rapidly–excites–and–energizes–an–audience."

Read *slowly:*
"A slow rate of speech creates a mood of awe and wonder."

POWER UP!

Add energy to your words. Breathe from your abdomen and read each phrase. Emphasize the underlined word.

"<u>Speech</u> is important."

"Speech <u>is</u> important."

"Speech is <u>important</u>."

Push a key word in a sentence to add emphasis and interest.

THE VOICE—IT'S THAT GENDER THING

In voice development, there are some definite male and female differences.

Female Voices

Female voices are usually higher and less forceful. Women have historically been encouraged to speak softly. That doesn't work. What does work is getting some air in your lungs and pushing the sound out using a deliberate, firm voice. Don't *ask* for acceptance. *Expect it* in your tone of voice.

A woman at "Speech Camp" had a singsong, noncommanding voice. We asked her to role-play the part of a courtroom lawyer. Her voice variety was compelling. The change was dramatic. She said the following:

Voice exercise.

"My client is not guilty. (*Pause.*) She is a <u>mother</u> (*loud*), a businesswoman (*softly*), and a healer. We have eye-witnesses who will <u>swear</u> that she was in Chicago on the night of the murder. (*Fast.*) And . . . she was there (*slow and deliberate*) to see . . . her <u>first</u> grandchild born."

Voice variety is power from within. Breathe deeply from the abdomen, not from the chest. Push and practice to increase your comfort level with voice variety.

Male Voices

Men, on the other hand, often take on a *presentation persona*. The result is a firm, serious, male monotone. Many men retreat from the spirited people they are, to a droning dispenser of facts and figures. The passion ebbs; the listener becomes comatose.

Change the pace with dialogue. Begin by setting the scene: "Last night, around midnight the phone rang. I fumbled for the phone and heard the panicky voice of Sam, the night engineer. 'The pipes burst and the showroom is flooding. What should I do about the UPS packages stacked by the delivery room door?' " Dialogue changes the pace of the presentation and keeps the listener tuned in.

Voice exercise.
Emphasize one word in a sentence to add interest and impact. Don't be afraid to *whisper* a word or a phrase. It's not *wimpy.* It is *powerful* and *draws* the listener to you. Pause to create tension . . . to build a-n-t-i-c-i-p-a-t-i-o-n.

BE CONVERSATIONAL

Use a conversational style, if you need a written text of your presentation. Use short sentences. To quote Joe Plumeri, the president of Primerica Financial Services, a fine and *passionate* [his word] communicator, "I never give a speech, I give a chat."

SOUND LIKE YOU MEAN IT

Listeners want to hear interesting speakers who show conviction about their messages. Speakers often think using a wide range of voice variety is being too dramatic, or acting. Actually, without voice variety, listeners can't tell advantages from adversity. Droning numbs the ear and acts like Novocain for the mind.

A young lawyer stood out among the other litigators in a workshop. He spoke with great conviction. He was quiet and sincere. His voice grew loud and emphatic. He paused . . . to force us to think about what he had said. His mock presentation to the jury was impressive because of the tension and the energy in his voice. When asked what it takes to speak with such confidence and conviction, his answer was, "Courage."

> **"**I didn't get the job in the Domino's Pizza commercial because I was pretty—I'm sure they had a million girls who were pretty. I got it because I was convincing in the audition. When I ate my pizza, *that* pizza was *really* good.**"**
>
> —Alicia Silverstone, actress, *Clueless*

YOU WANT TO DO *WHAT?*
INFLECTION

Can you imagine Clint Eastwood ending his famous saying, "Make my day," with an upward inflection?

Stamp out a singsong voice. Read this sentence and raise your voice at the end: "The company was founded in 1988." Raising it sounds like a question. Now read it and inflect downward. Now that's a fact.

A downward inflection at the end of a phrase, a sentence, or even a question implies authority. "What do you think ↑?" "What do you think ↓?"

AEROBICIZE YOUR LIPS: ARTICULATE

Stamp out lazy lips and valley girl lockjaw. Lazy lips and a tight jaw cause mumblers and mutterers. Open your mouth and exercise your lips.

EXERCISE 1: USE A TAPE RECORDER

Communication guru Roger Ailes suggests speakers try the "Tape and Ape" method. Tape a segment on radio or TV. Transcribe it and read it into a recorder. Play it back and compare. Do it again.

Read a sentence into your tape recorder with a frown on your face. Now read it with a smile. Play them both. Can you *hear* your smile?

Tape your own telephone conversation or a conversation with a coworker. If you don't have a tape recorder leave a long message on your answering machine or your voice mail. Listen to your voice as if you were a client, your boss. How do you come across? Make a list of the qualities you like and the things you'd like to work on.

EXERCISE 2: LOWER THE PITCH OF YOUR VOICE

When you are nervous, the muscles that pull on your vocal chords tighten. Your breathing becomes shallow, from the chest, not the abdomen. Your pitch goes up.

Try this exercise to relax the vocal chords. Put a pencil between your teeth. Bite down forcing your back teeth apart as you speak. This forces you to drop your jaw and automatically lowers your voice. Practice it.

VOICE POWER

Your voice can convey conviction, excitement, energy, anger, sadness, joy—the full range of emotions. It is a powerful, easy-to-use tool to motivate individuals or groups. Your voice can move a listener to action, forge a commitment, rally the troops.

Warm up your voice before you make that million dollar presentation. Take a breath, yawn, and breath. Think, "*Yes!*" It will give your voice energy and your message enthusiasm.

RECAP

MO: Voice energy motivates listeners.

→ Add spice. Change the pace: loud, soft, slow, and fast.

→ Open your mouth. Enunciate your words.

→ Sound like you mean it. If you don't sound like you care, why should the listener?

> **"** Nothing great was ever accomplished without enthusiasm.**"**
> —Ralph Waldo Emerson

II

The Pause That Impresses

You could hear it in his voice. Tension. Anticipation.
He held them in suspense. . . . His control was intense.
He knew the power of the pause.

"**B**ond . . . James Bond," knows the incredible power of the pause
over foes, females, or felons. The power of silence is gripping.
The problem for most speakers is that a pause may grip the listener, but to the speaker it feels like the silence lasts forever. The listener, on the other hand, barely notices the pause, but responds to its effect.

Actor Kelsey Grammer, of *Cheers* and *Frasier,* says of his hero Jack Benny, "He was one of the greatest comedians because he was not afraid of pausing, not afraid of the silence."

The pause is power . . . *control.* The power to:

Build anticipation and tension.

Emphasize a key word or thought.

Collect your thoughts.

Replace filler words, such as *uhms, ers,* and *buts.*

Breathe.

Let your listener absorb your thought. . . . This idea may mean money in your pocket.

And all this high-octane power is at your disposal! The following techniques and situations will show you how and when to make it your own.

Read and record this sentence:

> A pause shows poise . . . control . . . *confidence*. . . . Use it. . . . *Master it.*

Reread (counting the pause dots silently) and record it until you can hear a discernible difference. Count silently to four to insure that you extend the terrifying pause.

Train your ear to become comfortable with silence. Practicing and owning this skill can make an instant impact in your every communication. A young lawyer noted that a partner in the firm rudely ignored him when he was reporting on his findings. A colleague suggested, "Pause when she won't acknowledge you. She'll look up."

NO ONE TALKS TOO FAST

Have you ever been told you talk too fast . . . or felt that others do? The average person speaks at 175 words per minute. We can listen to over 300 words per minute. No one speaks too fast, in fact, people tend to think you are smarter if you speak a bit faster. Motivational sales speaker Zig Ziglar, says that he speaks at 225 words per minute with gusts up to 550.

The problem is, that in your race from sentence to sentence your ideas don't have the time to take root. The solution is *the pause*. It gives the listener's brain time to compute thoughts and ideas.

"The pause that refreshes."
—The Coca-Cola Company

Ask a friend to give you his telephone number as quickly as possible. Try writing it down. Try it again. This time, have your friend add a pause or two and you will get it on the first read.

POWER PAUSE EXERCISES

Read and observe this TV TelePrompter copy. The anchor marked the script by underlining the words to emphasize and adding a slash to indicate a pause. These indications make the copy conversational. Notice that sentences are short.

ORGAN BANK/FEDERAL
GUIDELINES pwh noon 3/10
  LIVE

AII   (PATRICIA)

   AN <u>ATLANTA</u>
ORGAN BANK IS BEING
TOLD TO <u>SHAPE UP</u>
OR BE <u>DROPPED</u> FROM
THE NATIONAL
NETWORK. //

VO ENG

(VO) <u>LIFELINK</u> OF
GEORGIA COORDINATED
THE <u>DISTRIBUTION</u>
OF THE ORGANS
INVOLVED IN LAST
WEEKEND'S "DONOR
ORGAN <u>TRANSPLANTS</u>"
AT <u>EMORY</u>. //
   A <u>SPECIAL</u> PANEL
SAYS THE ORGANIZATION
IS <u>NOT</u> FOLLOWING
FEDERAL GUIDELINES/
IN DISTRIBUTING
SCARCE DONOR ORGANS.

PAUSE TO LET YOUR
LISTENERS CATCH UP

It is the absence of the pause, not high-speed delivery that causes a speaker to lose the listener.

Think of asking a friend to follow you in her car. If your friend gets caught at a red light, you pull over and pause until she is behind you again. That is the essence of the pause. It gives the listener time to catch up and absorb your data.

PAUSE TO CLOAK NERVOUSNESS

> **"Fake it til you make it."**

We tend to race when we are ill at ease and give a prospect a tornado of information. Breathe. A conscious pause before you begin helps you appear calm and confident, with everything under control. It's a "*fake it til you make it*" technique. Continue to pause and breathe before you make an important statement. This will both increase your sense of control and your presence.

PAUSE TO ELIMINATE
THE KNOCKS AND PINGS

Ands, ehs, buts, OKs, and *ya knows* are filler words that distract and detract from your message. Break this habit. It may not be harmful to your health, but it damages your image as a leader.

Instead of idling in communication traffic, come to a complete stop. Don't open your mouth until your thought is in gear and you are ready to say the

next sentence. A smooth, confident pause eliminates engine clogging *ers*. The president of a large,
international organization stood at the podium. His
words were thoughtful, but there was an *er* in every
sentence. In a matter of minutes he had lost his
impact and his listeners.

PAUSE TO HIGHLIGHT SALES POINTS

A group of salespeople in real estate wanted an
edge in making winning sales presentations.

Because they were so comfortable with their
information and the key points of the property,
they tended to fire-hose their delivery. We encouraged them to pause to emphasize each key sales
point and add impact to their pitch.

> "The property is surrounded by houses that sold
> for well over $150,000. (*Pause.*) The average
> household income in that area is more than
> $100,000. (*Pause.*) The traffic for each store in
> the area is second only to Henry Mall."

Use your pause effectively to let your listeners feel
the impact of each selling point.

PAUSE PLUS

The pause is uncomfortable until it becomes your
habit. Challenge yourself. Make it a game to use the
pause to grow as a communicator. As Mark Twain
said, "There is nothing so powerful as the rightly
timed pause."

> "There is
> nothing so
> powerful as
> the rightly
> timed pause."
> —Mark Twain

RECAP

MO: The pause is the ultimate tool of the confident communicator.

→ Pause to control your audience. They'll look up and wonder what you're going to say.

→ Pause to emphasize a point. Pause before and after you make a point.

→ Pause to eliminate the *ands, ehs,* and *buts.*

12
Dump the
Distractions

When you're interested in attracting the trust and confidence of a key decision maker, dump the distractions. Distractions confuse and annoy.

During the 1992 presidential campaign, critics suggested that Tipper Gore lose weight and that Hillary Clinton completely change her image as an outspoken workingwoman.

For Ms. Clinton and Ms. Gore, making changes came down to determining that the long-term goal was more important than the distracting details that the public chose to focus on. Like the wives of the candidates, you can ask a colleague to be objective and clue you in to your distractions.

Republican communications strategist Roger Ailes says, "You are the message." Make sure the impression you make doesn't sabotage your goals.

PHYSICAL DISTRACTIONS

Nervous habits including playing with change in your pocket, playing with pencils, or overgesturing can undermine your leadership goals.

> **"How do you prepare for a press conference? First you go to the hairdresser. Your family and friends don't care what you ask but they notice how you look."**
>
> —Helen Thomas,
>   *United Press International,*
>   Dean of White House Correspondents

Look like a vice president if you want to be one. Dress and grooming count. In the movie, "Working Girl," Melanie Griffith changed her image by wearing less makeup, a simpler hairstyle, and a professional wardrobe as she went from pool secretary to corner office executive.

Do your homework when choosing and coordinating your wardrobe. Look for role models in your own business, in magazines, or on TV.

Business dress is generally about conformity, even on casual days—so, if those are the rules . . . conform, but with quality. Even casual impressions count!

VERBAL DISTRACTIONS

Verbal distractions include the *and, eh, buts, OKs,* and *you knows.* The cure is to replace the filler words with a pause.

Mumbles and monotones and voices that die out at the end of a sentence are distractions that cause a listener to tune you out. How do you sound on your answering machine or voice mail? Would you look forward to talking to that person? Open your mouth and enunciate. Emphasize a word in each sentence to add energy. Listen to the playback.

Accents do not distract if you open your mouth, enunciate, and pause. Former Texas governor Ann Richards is an enthusiastic celebration of a Texas accent.

PSYCHOLOGICAL DISTRACTIONS

Psychological distractions cause people to tune out your message. "People tend to dislike or mistrust people whose ideas are different than their own," said Josephine Britton, former English teacher at the Loomis Chaffee School in Windsor, Connecticut.

The more you are like your listener the easier it is to make the connection. Psychologists recommend modeling and mirroring a listener's behavior.

Pace your rate of speech to the speed of your listener. People in different parts of the country speak at different rates. Mirroring their speech will help you to strengthen the connection and build a relationship.

A Coca-Cola marketing executive explained that, as a newcomer to Atlanta, his northern accent and fast-paced conversation wasn't helping him build the cooperation he needed with peers and colleagues. By mirroring the pace and energy of others, he softened his image and strengthened his relationships.

Similarly, Hillary Clinton became more sensitive to the attitudes of people unfamiliar with her workingwoman lifestyle. Her message was heard once she became sensitive to her listeners and focused on the interests that they had in common.

RECAP

MO: Foil your detractors—avoid distractions.

→ Physical distractions compete with your information.

→ Verbal distractions including monotone and filler words turn your listener off.

→ Psychological distractions arc usually founded on the listener's prejudices. The more you can fit in with the listeners, the more likely they will be to hear you.

13

It Was One of Those Electric Moments: Microphones

Mike fright can jump-start that quivering, shaking feeling. A presentation with a microphone can be heart stopping, whether it's for the financial community or the PTA.

With know-how you can ramp up your voltage and generate power from the podium.

STAND AWAY

"People either lean in and EAT THE MIKE or they stand back and can't be heard," says Steve Shipley, operations manager with Georgia-based Corporate Audio/Visual. You should be between eight and twelve inches away from the microphone.

It's important to speak directly toward a podium mike. Think of it as taking a drink from a water fountain: The water doesn't come to you—you have to move the mike to the direction of your mouth. The mike is just below your mouth.

Go early and practice. "Most people aren't accustomed to speaking into a mike and expect too much from themselves," said Pat Marcus, producer and disc jockey from Atlanta's STAR 94FM.

"Every mike feels and works differently. I do a sound-check beforehand so I know where to stand, how to position the mike and get used to the sound."

Take control. Before you speak, reach up and adjust the mike. Inevitably the five-foot-three presenter follows the six-foot-two speaker and there's not a chance in the world that the person will be heard if he or she doesn't have the guts to reposition the mike. If you can, call ahead and ask for a lavalier microphone to wear so that you can move away from the lectern.

DON'T GET CAUGHT AMPLIFYING A DULL, LITTLE VOICE

Get over the sound of your own voice. Take the gumption to power up before your key messages are carried through a mike. Low voltage at the podium is often the result of the shock of hearing your voice amplified for the first time.

Others lose voltage because they try to speak in a well-modulated, reserved voice. Without muscle you can't tell the main issues from the subpoints. You don't have a clue whether the statements made are fact or merely promises of things to come.

Exaggerate the highs, the lows, and the pauses. Think big. Get some breath behind your voice. Know your first sentence cold. Be bold and in control. Imagine how actor Anthony Hopkins or poet Maya Angelou would deliver your information.

Look at the size of the room and think of how far you would have to throw a ball to hit the back wall. Do the same with your voice. Pause, take a breath from your gut. Then power up your voice to fill the space. Don't let a buyer or decision maker fail to catch your message.

RECAP

MO: Make the mike work for you.

→ Go early and practice with the mike.

→ Stand eight to twelve inches away to avoid distortion.

→ Adjust the mike. Bring it just below your mouth.

14

We're Going to Do It Again Until We Get It Right

It takes practice. Hardly anyone gets it right the first time. But a video camera lets you sit in your own audience and view your presentation as others do.

Each of us is a *work in progress* when it comes to presenting. Over time, we continue to change, adapt, and improve. Video practice and rehearsals can speed up the process.

Bill Liss, business reporter for WXIA-TV in Atlanta reviews his tapes after every show. "I came from a business background and knew I had a lot to learn about how I came across on the air," he said.

In these six on-camera exercises you will learn to look confident and sound conversational. When you rehearse a presentation in the quiet of your own home, don't be afraid to repeat the exercises until you become the presenter you want to be. Think of communication as your new sport, to get good at it—you need to practice. (It is easier than golf.)

Watch your tape as a boss, peer, client. Evaluate your performance from each of these points of view.

As a do-it-yourself coach, it's important to see how you look when you look your best. Often we

> " Oh, wad some power the giftie gie us To see oursel's as ithers see us! "
>
> —Robert Burns

work with clients before a job or a partnership interview. Knowing what it takes to produce the look of confidence—an open presence, strong eye contact, a smile, and a calm convincing voice—means that you can reproduce it on command.

LIGHTS, ACTION, ON-CAMERA EXERCISES

The following exercises build confidence. Work on *one* skill at a time. Review chapters 6 through 12 when you need a boost. Take risks. Be bold. Role-play to see if there is a more convincing and powerful you yearning to get free. You will be surprised and proud of the presenter you will become.

Create your own audience. Put yellow Post-its on the backs of chairs around the room or tear out pictures of different faces from magazines. Blow them up on the copier, cut them out, and tape them to the wall. Get them out of the closet whenever you need a practice audience. The faces give you eyes to focus on as you move about the room.

POSTURE EXERCISE: VIDEO

Exercise 1

✔ Stand in front of the video. Balance on the balls of your feet, chest up, arms at your side. Make eye contact with individuals.

✔ Talk for 30 seconds to a minute about your job. Use the Speechworks Formula.

✔ Do the exercise again talking about your favorite vacation spot.

Example
MO: For fun in a foreign land, choose Cancun.

It's close by air.

The language is easy.

The weather is glorious!

Elaborate and recap.

Exercise 2

Now do the same exercises seated at a desk.

Do you look more convincing when you talk about your vacation spot or your job?

Daily Practice

Stance
Turn your wait for an elevator, the grocery checkout, or the auto tag line into an opportunity to practice your stance. No one will know what you're doing and you can learn the feel of a confident presence.

Seated position
When you are on the phone at your desk, sit up, lean forward, and pretend that the caller is across the desk.

FACIAL EXERCISE

Exercise 3

Talk for 30 seconds about your vacation without using any expression.

Now, repeat the message. Smile, use your eyebrows and you will see that you look pleasant and not nearly as outrageous as you feel.

Learning to smile and talk at the same time is tough for many people. Yet a smile is a great disarmer and it signals confidence. A serious face merely looks anxious, not necessarily professional or confident.

Daily Practice

Practice smiling and lifting your eyebrows every morning as you shave or put on makeup. You will find that you look more energized than you thought and not nearly as dorky as you imagined.

EYE CONTACT EXERCISE: VIDEO

Exercise 4

✔ Talk about a report you are working on.

✔ Stand in front of the camera.

✔ Make eye contact with members of your audience.

Give a whole thought to each person (object) for three to five seconds.
There is a natural tendency to pause as you speak to each new face. This gives listeners a "for-your-eyes-only" feeling.

GESTURE AND MOVEMENT: VIDEO

Exercise 5

Describe your office or favorite room with your hands and arms. Physically take listeners to your door, window, bookcase, phone, etc. Make firm, exaggerated gestures to give you a more open and in-control look. All gestures are forward. Hold the gesture. . . .

Daily Practice

You can practice every skill except eye contact while talking on the phone. Stand up and gesture. Walk around your chair. Practice facial energy. Put a mirror by your phone; a smile on your face puts a smile in your voice.

VOICE EXERCISE: VIDEO/AUDIO

Exercise 6

Role-play each of the following exercises. Step out of yourself and take risks with each role to see a more powerful you.

The purpose of this exercise is to experiment with voice variety, to practice new skills, and to take risks in order to reap rewards. Think about pausing, emphasising a word, speaking loud or soft, fast or slow. Project from your toes. Do 40 seconds impromptu on a character and then review. Try it again. Try another one.

- ✔ A lawyer at the end of a trial making an emotional plea to the jury to find guilty/free the defendant. Use pauses.
- ✔ A coach motivating the losing team at half-time.
- ✔ A drill sergeant dressing down the troops.
- ✔ An angry CEO taking command of a messy corporate situation.
- ✔ A citizen bringing a cause before the city council.

Change the pace: pause, fast, slow, loud, soft.

Daily Practice

Practice on the phone and in the mirror. Once you see yourself with more power and energy, you won't leave home without it. Get naked. Get in the shower and articulate your words. The echo in the bathroom will enhance your voice projection.

RECAP

MO: Practice and grow in confidence.

→ Choose one skill to practice. It takes 21 days to change a habit. Choose and focus on one element: your voice energy, eye contact, or the pause. Then move on to work on another facet of your communication skills.

→ Practice daily. Practice on the phone, in meetings, and in conversation.

→ Rehearse on camera. The CEO of a major optical company keeps a video camera set up in his basement for practice.

PART 3

WINNING

Woo and win! Now that you've learned the basics, the Speechworks Formula, and all the right moves, it's time to test this wooing and winning strategy and build long-term relationships in all the right places: team presentations, meetings, seminars, on the phone, and, *gulp,* in impromptu speaking situations.

This section shows you:

✔ What kind of W&W strategy it takes to win a team presentation
✔ How to use interactive participation to involve your seminar participants
✔ What turns people on in a meeting
✔ How the Formula works for a job interview
✔ How to speak with self-assured confidence in an impromptu situation

The more successful you are in using the Wooing and Winning Strategy, the more valuable you become to yourself and others.

15

Red-Hot Competition: Team Presentations

A Big Six accounting firm team was attempting, against great odds, to take a 20-year client away from another Big Six firm. Speechworks was their coach. They followed the Formula exactly. They produced boards that highlighted the main points with cartoons. One of the three points, "We'll be with you on a rainy day," was reinforced with a drawing of a man in a yellow slicker.*

The team rehearsal built their confidence, their continuity, and their spirit. They planned to meet on the morning of the presentation at 7:30 A.M. at a McDonald's for one last pregame pep rally.

The team won the account. It was, as they wrote, "A big win for us." Similarly, it was a big win for Speechworks. They had a wooing and winning strategy focused on the buyer, supported by eye-catching visuals,* and rehearsals that created a great and lasting first impression.

Their team did it right, and so can yours.

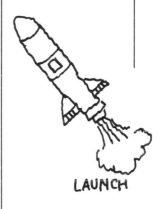

LAUNCH

---

* A low-tech, low-stress, approach using foam core boards plus simple cartoons is a winner. Neatness and professionalism is important, high tech isn't.

IT'S A RACE TO THE FINISH

Entrepreneurs, corporations, professionals, and even nonprofits are on the chase for business. Twenty-seven architectural firms compete for a major expansion of a hospital. Sixty-two law firms compete for a multimillion dollar international account. A myriad of emerging high-tech companies continually chase a small bevy of investors.

When the competition is swarming and there are red-hot suitors in on the chase, you need a wooing and winning team presentation strategy. If your client suddenly becomes the darling of other eager suitors, you have to fire up the commitment and be more appealing than ever.

After months of courting a prospect, you know its needs, its unique place in the industry, and how you can solve its problems. When you make the short list, the decision often comes down to how well your team presents itself and its message in that 30-minute presentation.

HOW TO BE A STANDOUT
IN A SHOOT-OUT

Think six o'clock news. Like the highly competitive TV news team, you have less than 30 minutes to give your listeners news they can use and get them to make your team their choice.

News team members constantly edit down stories to beat the clock. In your presentation, you'd like to have an hour to wow the prospect with your company's accomplishments. Your listeners only want a 20- to 30-minute explanation of how you can cure their headache. Focus on their needs, not your story, to keep them tuned in and achieve success.

GET A NEWS PRODUCER

Team presentations, like news programming, are events that are ripe for dissension, riddled with internal politics, constant change, and mounting tension. Panicky presenters and unfocused presentations are the result.

Take a tip from news assignment editors who, with the news producer and reporters, put together live programs daily. Get a leader, the company president, or project leader, who can pull together the list of points that will give your show credibility and high ratings.

The morning meeting in the newsroom is open for brainstorming and discussion on which stories to cover, but all final decisions rest with one person. Reporters may beg for an extra 30 seconds for their stories. They pout over losing a juicy story to another member of the news team. You saw it happen on *Murphy Brown*. Frank, Murphy, and Corky are often at odds on who gets the good story—but Miles, the producer, rules.

THE CORPORATE MESSAGE

Begin with the Message Objective, the lead story. What's in it for the listener to do business with you? Determine the key points.

The asset management team of a large international real estate firm made a presentation to the owner of an office complex in Tampa, Florida, to get the management contract for his facility. Corporate leaders put pressure on the team to use the firm's size, age, prestigious Fortune 100 clients, and a high-tech slide presentation to impress the client.

All very nice. But as a reader you probably see the error of this thinking. Put yourself in the buyer's shoes. What would the building owner want?

The Listener-Centered Message

Speechworks encouraged the team to make a more buyer-focused presentation. The office complex owner wanted service, experienced management, and tenant occupancy.

The team gave examples of dedicated service and emphasized that 75 percent of the firm's clients were the same size or smaller than the prospect. They highlighted its size only as a resource to find local as well as international tenants. The listener-centered focus won the contract.

SEPARATE YOUR TEAM FROM THE COMPETITION

Follow the lead of local news stations who compete for viewers and ratings: Know the competition. What are their strengths? Who are their stars? How can you highlight your team's talents in ways that will show that you are clearly different and better?

The partners in the health care practice at Alston & Bird, Atlanta's largest law firm, are young. They knew that their competitors would bring their highest-profile partners to the presentation. They, on the other hand, positioned themselves as the actual team that would manage and guide the job if awarded the work. They won.

BUILD CREDIBILITY

If it's the truth, it's not bragging. Lawyers, accountants, bankers, and engineers are reluctant to use success stories in team presentations for fear of bragging. When promoting themselves and their team, they prefer to use generalities when specifics make the sale.

Award-winning architect Stanley Daniels of Jova, Daniels, Busby, related a university student's comment to support his point about satisfied clients. "I was walking across the campus when a student recognized me as the architect. He said he was a senior and had the use of the new student sports center for only one year. He talked about what a boost the Center had been to campus spirit and morale. He thanked me." Daniels called that the kind of reward the client would be proud of.

If your company has clients who are raving fans, has achieved repeat business with its major clients, or provided on-time delivery every day, let those achievements speak for your team's capabilities. Real successes aren't bragging—they are facts and build credibility. These success stories make the decision maker say, "Yes. We need a team who can do that for our company."

We recently heard three public relations firms pitch business for a large nonprofit in Atlanta. Each gave a general capability presentation and some general ideas of what they would do if they won the account. Only one gave a specific suggestion the foundation could relate to and then backed it up with a specific example of how the project had worked in a commercial enterprise. They won the competition.

We can't say it enough. *Specifics* speak louder than generalities.

USE VISUALS TO MAKE YOUR TEAM MEMORABLE

Gardner Coursen, a partner with the law firm of Glass, McCullough, Sherrill and Harrold, has first-hand experience with the power of graphics in a team presentation. "We were successful because we used a simple graphic to show how our team would attack a very complex problem."

Follow TV's rule for visuals. Use color, pictures, and graphics to excite the eye and invite curiosity. Imagine the impact of a team that makes a buyer sit

"Don't kill your listeners with Bullets."

—Speechworks

through endless bulleted slides versus the team that uses interesting pictures and imaginative graphics. "You can never bore anybody into buying anything" is a Speechworks motto.

Make the prospect feel important. Marry your logo with their logo to enhance your off-the-shelf presentation. Determine your key points and brainstorm to create a memorable visual that connects you visually to the prospect.

Sometimes the presentation team needs to go all out. We worked with four construction companies who made a joint venture presentation to build the Georgia Dome. Their presentation opened with an exciting football video (the Hook), and then the principals (anchors) led off with the Preview, followed by senior managers, estimators, and project managers (the reporters).

Their visuals were eight-by-twelve-foot blowups mounted on foam core which served as a unique background. The presentation closed after the Q&A with gifts of NFL footballs signed by each key member of the construction team. The 30-minute presentation had the energy and the news value of a network broadcast.

They won the $150 million contract. You saw the results in Super Bowl XXVIII.

CLOSE WITH CONVICTION

In team presentations, the leader recaps the Message Objective, the three main points, and asks for the prospect's order at the end of the presentation. This is no time to be coy and hope the buyer knows your team is interested.

PLAN FOR QUESTIONS AND ANSWERS

Plan for the very bad, worst, terrible questions your team could be asked. Ask each team member to come up with three easy and three tough questions. Get questions from outsiders with more of a prospect's point of view. Take turns answering them. Get team input to improve the answers. During the presentation, the leader will take the questions or field them to the expert. Close with the leader recapping and again asking for the order.

Facing the worst possible questions in the comfort of your office will be far easier than in an unfamiliar board room. . . . And when you hear them ask the question you expected, you'll get that confident "*Yes!*" feeling.

BEWARE OF LATE-BREAKING NEWS

The CEO of one architectural firm constantly changed the presentation up to show time. This is doable with an experienced news team, but unsettling and counterproductive for most business team presenters.

ADOPT A NEWS TEAM LINEUP

TV anchors open the program, lead off with highlights, and close the show. Reporters fill in with updates from their fields of responsibility. Make similar team assignments. The senior member of your team is an anchor and introduces the team after the Hook, Message Objective, and Preview

❝Everyone has the will to win. But do you have the will to prepare?❞

—Bill Curry,
football coach,
University
of Kentucky

have been stated. The anchor would then say, "I'm here with _____, an expert in computer law. . . ." to introduce individual team members.

REHEARSE TO ADD TEAM POLISH

Would you tune in to a news team that read the stories, looked at the floor, fidgeted with their hands, or talked too long? No. The anchors you watch are confident, conversational, and, above all, practiced.

Establish a sacred, minimum three-hour rehearsal rule. No practice—no pitch. Most teams hate to practice. They would rather screw up in front of a client than rehearse in front of teammates. Coworkers are quick to criticize, slow to praise. Clients are silent. But they vote with dollars.

Set up a video camera and record the entire presentation. Then ask team members to sit back and evaluate it as though they were buyers. This rehearsal gives each team member a sense of familiarity with the whole message and how each of their parts fit in. It cuts out overlap and reduces logistical problems with presentation order, slides or overheads, and the close.

❝It's not perfection, it's connection.❞
—Speechworks

Look for mannerisms that could distract from the message. Do you work together well as a team? Do you honor each other's time? Do you show interest when others speak? The goal is to be caring and conversational . . . *connection* not *perfection*. Too slick is a turnoff. Weak presenters improve with practice.

After a full rehearsal, do a transition run through. Team members should practice their own open/close and transition to the next presenter. A confident, predetermined, well-spoken open and close eliminates rambling and adds to your credibility.

TV news team members know exactly how long their segments will run. Team presenters need the same discipline. They say they hate to talk, but once they get on their feet, they just can't seem to shut up. Ramblings

---

REHEARSAL CHECK SHEET

Rate your presentation like a prospect.

1. Do they have a good understanding of our needs? Do they understand the unique role we play in our industry? WII-FM?

2. Have they worked with similar clients?

3. Have they worked with our target markets previously?

4. How do you rate the quality of their work?

5. Who will be working with us (our contacts) and what is their experience?

6. Do they have a balanced team? Are they strongly staffed in the areas we need?

7. Was their presentation well organized and directed to our specific needs?

8. Do they have rapport with each other and with us?

9. Do they have the staff, hardware, physical facilities to handle our business?

10. Is the management solid? Does it have a long-term point of view?

11. Is there something different about them that matches up with our current and future needs?

12. Is there a process to evaluate progress? Is there a method in place to measure success?

ruin relationships, create angst among teammates, and devastate presentation timing.

RATE YOUR PRESENTATION LIKE A PROSPECT

Ratings are everything to the news team. Similarly, you will be rated in your presentation.

A strong benefit, compelling support points, and interesting examples address prospects' needs. A conversational, confident delivery by your team tells them about the synergy and strength of the team.

Use the Rehearsal Check Sheet on the previous page to make team rehearsals on target.

RECAP

MO: Be a winner!

→ Think TV news—get a news producer, anchors, and reporters to make your team stand out in a shoot-out.

→ Get organized—Brainstorm ideas, develop a structure, create visuals, and plan for Q&A.

→ Rehearse—as if your cash flow depended on it!

16
Seminars That Sizzle and Sell

As a favorite mentor says to us, "People do business with people they like and trust. In order to trust you, they have to get to know you, and that takes time." A seminar is a time to begin that process.

Build curiosity. Create a lust for learning. Give the attendees at your seminar a sample of how you or your company has been a problem solver for others, and they will follow you anywhere.

To be successful, you don't have to be Tony Robbins or Zig Ziglar, but you do have to follow a formula for success, or risk wasting your time and money.

DEFINE THE AUDIENCE AND
HOW YOU CAN ATTRACT IT

Figure out the niche you want to serve. One financial consultant targeted retirees because they were accessible. Unlike business owners or physicians, they open their mail and answer their own phones.

Renee Brody Levow, of the senior 401K advisory group at The Robinson-Humphrey Company, targets corporate accountants and CFOs in public and private companies who offer or plan to initiate 401K plans.

Like most niche seminars, Ms. Levow uses direct mail to fill her seminars. She hires students to locate and input mailing lists, but she personally makes all follow-up calls. It is the personal contact that begins to build the relationship. There are *three* contacts before the prospect comes to the

seminar. Prospects receive an invitation. After a call for free tickets, they receive a note and a map. Two days before the seminar she calls to remind them.

LEARN FROM SEMINAR PROS

For 18 years Money Management Seminars in Portland, Oregon, has designed seminars for financial and sales professionals to help them develop clients. Their investor education seminars are held in three 2½ hour sessions with no sales pitch. They feel that three seminars build the relationship and trust between the financial consultant and the attendees. The fourth session, an optional meeting, is a private financial consultation. The $50 fee for the seminar and workbook is designed to attract committed participants.

The industry rule of thumb is that a targeted mailing list of 10,000 will attract a .03 percent return. . . . That is about twenty people. Of these, about 60 percent convert to customers. They also recommend offering two or three seminars at one time to make the most of the mailing and to offer make-up days for attendees.

TARGET YOUR PARTICIPANTS' NEEDS

What's in it for the listeners to attend? Will they increase sales, become more productive, invest more profitably, become more fit, learn to use a computer more efficiently?

We worked with a lawyer giving a seminar about issues concerning a new tax law. The information had all the makings of a technically dry monologue.

We recommended that he clearly identify the benefit to the listeners. He opened with a battle plan concept aimed at showing them how to maneuver through dangerous tax territory. He talked about three potential land mines and gave strategies for getting around each. He wooed and won the group with his lively approach to a deadly subject.

FILL-IN-THE-BLANK STUDY GUIDES REINFORCE YOUR INFORMATION

Use fill-in-the-blank study guides. They increase participant involvement and prevent competitors from stealing your information.

Instead of writing out your information, leave blank spaces. Attendees fill in the spaces as you supply the information. Invite them to stop you if you skip a section or if they are unsure about your information.

Use overheads to reinforce the study guide. Participants see, hear, and record as the instructor makes notes. Participation reinforces the learning.

Make sure your company name, phone number, and other relevant information are included on study guides and handouts to insure that prospects can make easy contact.

REHEARSE TO INSURE POLISH

Rehearsing gives you the confidence to give a high-energy, conversational presentation. It also gives you an overview of content, flow, and timing.

We moderated a small business owners seminar for Sprint. Each of the six panelists was limited to ten minutes to insure a well-paced session. We were tough timekeepers. A minute extra here and a minute extra there bores and batters listeners.

One of the presenters had far more information than time. Had he rehearsed, he would have been comfortably in control of his visuals, his information, and his time. As time ticked away, he had to fly through and toss out many of his overheads. He looked rushed and frantic and failed to make his point.

MAKE IT INTERACTIVE

Set up the room so that, as the speaker, you're an integral part of the audience. Podiums and platforms separate you from participants. Build in easy access to the group. Interactivity changes the pace and increases the level of interest.

A financial consultant involved participants by asking them to come up with a list of life's common expenses, rather than presenting his list to them. He wrote on the overhead as participants listed food, shelter, automobile, entertainment. As a result, participants interacted with him and each other. They felt that they had some control of their situation and he easily filled in any points they had missed.

To involve reluctant participants, divide a large group into small discussion groups of five or six. Ask a question or pose a situation and ask each group to discuss it. Following that, get feedback from a member of each group.

A Big Six accounting firm did an FSB109 tax seminar for their corporate clients. Rather than comparing the old and new methods, the seminar leader asked each table of participants to come up with comparisons by using the old and new tax methods in a specific exercise.

You will be surprised at the quantity and quality of information that comes from audience involvement. This involvement breaks down barriers and builds up relationships.

Bob Pike, president of Creative Training Techniques, is a master of interactive training techniques. He believes strongly in two concepts: That people believe their own information, and, as Confucius said, "What I hear, I forget. What I see, I remember. But what I do, I understand."

EVALUATE TO IMPROVE

Videotape your seminar to see yourself as participants do. Ask participants to fill out an evaluation at the end of the program. You'll get feedback on the subject, an evaluation of the quality of the presentation, and

SAMPLE SEMINAR EVALUATION FORM

NAME: _____   DATES: _____
     (*optional*)

In our constant efforts to improve our seminar, we greatly appreciate your responses to the questions and statements listed below. Please include any additional comments you may have.

1. What idea or concept will you take with you as a result of the seminar?

_____

_____

2. What would you like to see done differently?

_____

_____

3. How would you describe today's seminar to a colleague who is considering attending?

_____

_____

Please answer the following questions based on a 1 to 10 scale, with 10 being "very valuable" and 1 being "no value."

4. How valuable were the seminar's ideas and concepts to you? Please comment:

_____

_____

5. How would you rate the effectiveness of the presenter? Please comment:

_____

_____

SEMINAR CHECKLIST

Prepare

✔ *Know your stuff.*   You are an expert sharing your solutions to your listeners' problems. Use the formula to organize the seminar: preview, present, recap.

✔ *Know your audience.*   Get a list of attendees before the meeting if you are a guest speaker and did not generate the list. Call a few participants to research their needs.

✔ *Arrive early.*   Be visible, meet people, and stay late. The goal is relationship building. Come early to hear other speakers and relate to what they've said.

Persuade

✔ *Get close to your audience.*   Move away from behind the podium. Go back only to check notes.

✔ *Never read your presentation.*

✔ *Leave the lights up.*   Overheads and flip charts build relationships. Slides leave your audience in the dark.

✔ *Interact with the group.*   Ask questions. Generate participation.

✔ *Give it away.*   The more you tell how you solved the problem, the more participants think there is to know.

✔ *Give examples.*   Explain how you and your organization have solved problems for others in similar situations. These are subliminal commercials.

✔ *Answer questions as they come.*   Your comfort with Q&A scores points for you as a coach and problem solver. Supply 3×5 cards for personal questions that don't interest the whole group. Offer to respond to those at the break.

✔ *Get feedback at the break.*   Ask attendees why they came, if they are getting the information they need, or what's missing. Adjust to fulfill audience needs.

✔ *Have participants fill out an evaluation.*

Pursue

✔ *Send participants a thank you note for attending.*

✔ *Send follow-up information.*   If you discuss something at a break, send additional information or articles of interest later.

✔ *Call participants to ask for feedback on the seminar.*

✔ *Continue the relationships and win business.*

quotes that will help you promote the next seminar. Keep the evaluation to one page or risk irritating a listener who is anxious and ready to leave.

One seminar leader emphasized the importance of evaluations with the story about a competitor/heckler whose complaints to the university who sponsored him put him at risk of losing his prestigious seminar location. The positive reviews of the other participants' evaluations clearly disproved the challenge.

FOLLOW UP TO WIN

Seminar experts say that 25 to 60 percent of the opportunity to do business is lost by failing to follow up with attendees. Plan your follow-up strategy when you plan the seminar. Set up your follow-up as part of the seminar content. "I have a Six-Point Investment Guideline to help you make wise decisions. I will discuss this with you when I follow up."

RECAP

MO: Seminars build relationships that build business.

→ Prepare. Plan ahead to assure attendance and attention to details.

→ Persuade. Present with confidence and connect with your listeners by involving them in the seminar.

→ Pursue. Follow up to continue the relationship and solve problems for prospects.

17
The Secret to Getting Involved

Big talkers bore. The true wooer listens. Even the shyest or most reticent participant has thoughts, opinions, and experiences on any subject. Their contribution makes them a stakeholder in the information and the relationship. Make your presentations interactive and your intended will feel valued and important.

Now that you have a handle on the Formula and are comfortable with your presentation skills, use these interactive procedures to further enhance your success as a communicator. Interactive presentations work in sales presentations, meetings, seminars, workshops, new business presentations, or formal presentations. Have courage. It makes your target feel terrific.

THE WOOING DIFFERENCE

The president of a major hotel chain gave an inspiring workshop on leadership. He opened the session and hooked his audience by asking participants to list characteristics of leaders versus managers. He used the audience's criteria as the basis for his pre-

sentation. The discussion was lively, personal, and involving. The group had a stake in the information and took ownership of the findings.

Later that year, this executive read a keynote address on the same subject. Although the information was the same, the energy and vitality was missing. The audience was told, not involved. It listened rather than participated.

EVERYBODY'S DOING IT

TV programming is participatory. Donahue, Oprah, talk shows, game shows, and even the shopping networks show that audiences like to get involved. Talk radio attracts callers. Surfers on the Internet like to make contributions in their chat groups.

Engage a listener mentally, physically, and emotionally and you will cement a bond and insure a stakeholder's involvement in the outcome. Good salespeople know the rule, "Talk 25 percent. Listen 75 percent." Adopt this rule in your business presentation and build relationships that build profits.

Two attorneys from a large Atlanta law firm gave a three-hour continuing education seminar on legal motions for 70 administrative law judges (ALJs). The deadly subject became a participatory treat. The MO of the presentation was: "By understanding the motions, the justices would save time."

The attorneys opened the session by asking about common motions the judges encounter. There were several volunteers. Then one attorney introduced the ALJ's top ten motions (not to be mistaken for anything that David Letterman would have interest in).

The audience was seated at ten tables. Each table was given a hypothetical situation and asked to apply a specific motion. A volunteer from each group reported on the case. The attorneys highlighted the two major features of each motion on an overhead. If questions came up, the attorneys asked for input from the group. The senior judges enjoyed their role as contributing experts, and the session exceeded expectations.

The results:

Everyone learned more about specific motions.

The judges appreciated the involvement of peers.

The groups increased their body of knowledge on motions.

Their firm improved its relationship with the judges.

The attorneys felt the session was more productive and less work.

WHY PRESENTERS FEAR PARTICIPATION

Here are five excuses presenters use for not encouraging audience participation:

"I have too much to say."

"It's easier for me to just tell 'em."

"I'm more comfortable with lecture style."

"People will think I don't know my stuff."

"I'm afraid I'll lose control."

The real reasons are: "I don't know how to do it." "It's scary to ask for input." "What if no one says anything?"

Trust us. In ten years of interactive presentations, we have never had members of a group fail to respond. The real problem is trying to shut them up. Although you may cover less, the group will remember more. Individuals' input adds to the body of knowledge.

WHY INTERACTIVE PRESENTATIONS WORK
FOR PRESENTERS AND LISTENERS

Presenters

1. Changes the pace and holds listeners' attention.

2. Gives the presenter more time to think and regroup.

3. Increases buy-in. Groups that work to prove *their* ideas are winners. Audiences believe their own information more than yours.

4. Increases trust. The ability to interact builds relationships.

5. Adds humor and spontaneity through group feedback.

6. Uncovers new information which can be used in future presentations.

Participation means less work for you. It's easier to ask a question than to give the answer. You get credit for being smarter, braver, and making information more fun for everyone.

Listeners

1. Makes learning more relevant. Sharing experiences and problem-solving techniques increases listeners' ability to apply information to their job.

2. Involves listeners and breaks preoccupation with outside thoughts.

3. In group activities you offer shy members an opportunity to make contributions in small group discussions and outgoing participants an opportunity to present the group's findings.

4. Presents opportunity to move around, get more physical.

5. Builds coworker and group member relationships.

Your challenge is to do more than deliver information. It is to motivate the listener to remember, value, and act on your information. To be successful, determine what knowledge your participants bring to the seminar. Interaction is based on prior knowledge. Participants can't have a discussion on the best methods of advertising a product if they have no knowledge of advertising methods, costs, and target markets.

Start small. Do one activity in a presentation. Once you try it you'll be hooked. An interactive presentation is cause for applause.

NINE WAYS TO MAKE YOUR GROUPS MORE INTERACTIVE

1. *Questions and answers.* This is the most common form of interactivity. Do you ever hear the comment, "The presentation got interesting when the Q&A session began"?

2. *Icebreaker surveys for seminars.* A stockbroker made an interactive presentation to a group of prospects. He took a quick survey to give the group a sense of the similarities and differences that it shared on investing.

   He asked a group of questions that ranged from "How many of you invest in utility stocks?" and "How many of you have considered bonds?" to "How many of you are currently investing in international stocks?" The survey built connections and gave guidelines to shared experiences.

   Guidelines for surveys. Give your seminar participants a sense of their similarities and their differences simply through a show of hands. Ask a series of relevant questions that set up your subject.

   How many of you travel more than _____ miles a year?

   How many use an on-line service?

   How many of you have a written will?

3. *Jump-start your meetings.* As chair of the Red Cross Communication Committee, Atlanta executive Marie Dodd opened a meeting by

asking for ideas to promote the Holiday Blood Drive in Atlanta. She gave small groups three minutes. They came up with 11 ideas. Four were implemented within the next two weeks.

Get a group involved when you are waiting for key people to arrive at a meeting. Participants like the challenge. Those who get there on time feel important and involved. Those who get there late miss the fun, but not the critical information.

Guidelines for jump starts.   Ask questions such as:

Why do our customers buy from us?

What could be the most outrageous solution for this widget?

What would arouse curiosity in our buyers?

How could we get an article in the *Wall Street Journal* about this product?

What is the biggest weakness of this product?

4. *Create a do-it-yourself list at a dinner meeting.*
   We asked a group of Foundation Fellows at the University of Georgia to list places on campus where members use their communication skills. In less than five minutes they came up with a list of 40 places. The interaction was far more engaging and action-oriented than reading *our list* of the same 40 from a slide.

Guidelines for creating do-it-yourself lists.   Ask your seminar work group to create a list. Ask for as many ideas as possible on a certain subject in a limited amount of time. Record the list on an overhead or flip chart. This compliments your group's knowledge. Fill in any missing points. This activity can be used in a meeting, presentation, seminar, or luncheon speech.

5. *Use small group discussion to insure group support.*   Char Fortune, vice president with ARES Realty Capital, led a group discussion about how the entire ARES team could support a new business effort.

After explaining the details of the new business initiative, she asked members of each group to come up with a list of services and a success story that demonstrated their ability to deliver this service effectively.

At lunch, each group told its story. Members presented the problem, the solution, and the results. "Their stories and service ideas were motivating. The group left with enthusiasm and greater sense of responsibility for achieving the new initiative," she said.

Guidelines for small group discussions.   Divide groups of 10 to 50 into small groups of 3 to 6 people. Give the purpose and instruction. Stand back. Let them struggle; It's part of the learning, sharing process.

Discussion topic suggestions:

What problems do you have organizing your information?
What are the benefits of this new strategy to your division?
How can we market successfully on the Internet?

Guidelines for larger group discussions.   Divide groups of 50 to 200 into groups of 20. General discussions about topics that are relevant to the group's day-to-day work experience are more lively.

Discussion topic suggestions:

What are the benefits of networking?
What are the drawbacks?
List good networking opportunities.

Objections and solutions.   If the group is slow to start, ask a specific person, "What kind of networking do you do?" "How do you use your PC?"

6. *Brainstorming sessions in meetings or seminars.*   An advertising executive littered the table with travel magazines and folders. He opened a brainstorming session by asking for ideas to promote a country inn in West Virginia. He used the magazines to jump-start thoughts.

Doug Hall, author of *Jump Start Your Brain,* advocates using stimuli, props, visuals, books, magazines, toys, something interesting to spark a flow of ideas. A diverse group, he believes, offers a broader perspective and produces innovative ideas and solutions. One idea hitchhikes with another.

Get a fresh perspective on a new or nagging problem by brainstorming. Set off a chain reaction of ideas on any problem from increased productivity to alternative work schedules.

Guidelines for brainstorming.   Think visually about your problem and come up with a *stimuli,* a visual relevant to the problem. Try a screwdriver for reworking a product, or a Mickey Mouse watch for ideas on scheduling solutions.

Initiate the *no bad ideas* rule in the brainstorming process. Negativism stunts enthusiasm and input. Let the flow go. A bad idea may lead to a great one.

Have a recorder write the ideas on a flip chart. Make it fun and relaxing. Avoid brain-draining situations.

Stop the session when the flow ebbs.

7. *Prioritize topics for discussion or actions: the green dot vote (physical participation).*   We facilitated a workshop for the National Board of Junior Achievement. In order to prioritize the items for discussion, we posted the workshop agenda on the wall. Then we gave every committee member three green dots (peel and stick dots) and asked them to vote on the three agenda items of most interest to them.

In less than three minutes, we had prioritized the discussion items according to the group's interests and had given the participants an opportunity to move around.

Guidelines for using the green dot vote.   Participants are eager to vote for their preferences. Make sure you give clear instructions *before* you pass out the dots.

This exercise can be done to:

Prioritize brainstorming ideas

Determine the most critical problems

Determine new directions

Determine the most plausible solutions

8. *Switch teams to keep the group fresh and productive.* A real estate executive faced an almost comatose group that had been listening to a slide presentation in the dark for almost two hours. It was a time for action.

   She asked the group of 75 to stand up, count off by sevens, and then move to the table with the appropriate number. She gave the group members a chance to move and stretch before she began her presentation. It was a just-in-time strategy that wooed the crowd and won their admiration and best input.

   Guidelines for switching groups. Ask your group to stand and count off. All the fives go to table five, all of the ones move to table one.

   This same exercise can be done with birthdays. All November-December birthdays move to table one. All February-March move to . . . It's fun, informative and fast.

9. *Play picture charades.* Get your group to interact visually. A group of insurance salespeople were quick to act when we asked them to draw, rather than write, the products they sold. They created pictures of car wrecks, tornadoes, college diplomas, fires, damaged computers, and tombstones. Then we hung the drawings around the room. It was visually interesting, fun, and made the salespeople look at their everyday business with a fresh eye.

Guidelines for picture charades.   Get participants involved visually after a long verbal session. Divide into a small group and give each group a piece of flip chart paper. Ask the members to draw:

A picture of what *quality* means in terms of their product.

Visual pictures, *keepers,* of what they learned from the meeting, seminar, workshop.

Objections and solutions.   Speakers fear responses such as:

"I don't know how to draw."

"My work can't be visualized."

   This doesn't happen in a group activity for two reasons.

1. Someone will lead the way.
2. You said do it! You are the leader.

RECAP

MO: Interact to get listener buy-in.

→ Plan ahead. Act like a lawyer and know the answers before you ask the questions. Create examples that will jump-start the interaction.

→ Practice giving step-by-step directions that avoid confusion. Give time frames. Let them know how long an activity will take.

→ Act confident. Use your voice and movement to control the group.

18
We Have to Stop Meeting Like This: Meetings

Are your rendezvous with staff, clients, or prospects eagerly awaited, stimulating, provocative? Put your heart into planning a meeting that gets results. Create a beat-the-clock format. Stimulate input and watch productivity skip a beat.

Both leaders and participant have a role in making meetings memorable. Whether you plan the agenda or prepare a report, you share in the responsibility of keeping discussions on track and adding energy and pacing.

> **❝**Two of the biggest problems in America are making ends meet and making meetings end.**❞**
>
> —Robert Orben

THE LEADER'S ROLE

Agenda First

Use the Formula to set the agenda. What's the MO (motivator), the benefit of the meeting? Plan to give a preview and then take the team through the agenda. Conclude with a recap and call for action.

Get input on the agenda from participants—this strategy builds buy-in. Send out the agenda ahead of time so everyone is mentally prepared for the meeting.

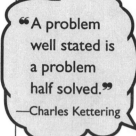

Start Fast

Hook 'em. Get participants involved quickly and
get their thinking juices flowing as the meeting
begins. Start with an attention getter, a story, a cartoon, a gee whiz fact, or an eye-opening statistic—
something dramatic or novel.

This strategy allows you to start on time, build in
a delay for stragglers, and avoid covering essential
material before the full group is present.

Open with a compelling question, break into
small groups, and give everyone two minutes to
come up with answers. "Why do companies buy
from us?" "What kind of community service project can we do that will build team morale and get
recognition for our organization?"

Establish Ownership in the Beginning

Let participants know how the meeting will impact
each of them. Your MO (motivator) could be: "We
will cover new ways of doing your jobs faster." Or,
"We'll talk about how to protect your health and
safety." Or, "Let's discuss profit-making potential
for the company and for you."

Change will occur faster if participants think the
meeting will impact their lives rather than just be an
airing for what's on your mind. Involvement creates
ownership in the change process. Participants need
to feel a sense of gain as a result of the meeting.

Use a Timed Agenda—Avoid Getting Sidetracked

Every group wants to adjourn on time. A timed
agenda builds group support for tabling discussions, sending problems back to committees, or
cutting off windbags.

Comments like, "In order to stay on track and get out by ten o'clock, I'd like Mary (or the marketing group) to study this problem and report on it next week," or, "We'd like to hear what you have to say, but in order for the group to be out on time we have to move on," will get cheers and support from the group.

If, on the other hand, a problem-solving session is going really well, the group could vote to continue and table another segment of the agenda.

Make the Meeting Interactive

Brainstorming sessions in meetings keep participants involved and allow the best and most profitable ideas to surface.

Charley Farley, president of Cohn & Wolf, an Atlanta public relations firm, says, "It's important not to criticize a person or idea in a brainstorming session. An off-beat suggestion can trigger 'the great idea.' Record all ideas on flip charts. Vote for the top three by having all attendees place color stickers on their top three choices. Discuss the pros and cons of the winners. Create an open, inviting environment for suggestions. Group input generates ownership and participants take responsibility for implementing the project or idea."

Recap and Review

Jimmy Calano and Jeff Salzman of the training seminar company Career Track, headline their meeting sessions, "Decisions, Dollars and Deadlines."

At the end of your meetings insure that your decisions, dollars, and deadlines actualize. Recap the action plans. Write them on a flip chart or chalkboard. Prioritize each item. Then ask partici-

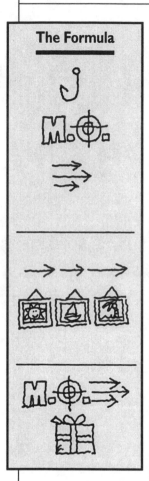

The Formula

pants to state their responsibility, the progress they intend to achieve, and the action steps they will take by the next meeting. Peer pressure of public promises produces action.

THE PARTICIPANT'S ROLE

Give a Fast-acting Report

TV reporters have no more than 90 seconds to give their report from city hall, Olympic headquarters, or the coliseum. If they can do it with cameras rolling, you can, too.

Use the Formula. Everyone asks Deborah Lane of Blue Cross–Blue Shield of Georgia and first woman president of the Columbus, Georgia, Chamber of Commerce, how she makes such succinct reports. She says, "I use the Formula."

The Formula will keep your report focused, convincing, and brief.

Get Buy-in Before the Meeting

"I had a report to present to the Board," said Cheryl Stephenson, assistant vice president of Southwire Company. "I was afraid that if the right people weren't behind me, no one would support the idea.

"I went to two key decision makers before the meeting and asked each to be my coach. I asked three questions. 'What was the history of the situation?' 'Why were others against it?' And finally, 'What would it take for him to support the idea?'

"All the work was done before the idea was presented. At the end of my report there were limited comments, good support and the idea was approved." Winning is about planning ahead.

MEETING QUESTIONNAIRE

Score 1 point for each *yes* answer and 2 points for each *no*

YES   NO

_____   _____   Did the meeting start on time?

_____   _____   Did everyone know specifically what was to be accomplished in the meeting?

_____   _____   Were the right people, rather than extraneous people, invited?

_____   _____   Was there a timed agenda?

_____   _____   Did the meeting stay on track?

_____   _____   Did participants make concise reports?

_____   _____   Did they get buy-in for their ideas?

_____   _____   Were visuals used effectively in the meeting?

_____   _____   Did the meeting end on time?

_____   _____   Did the group leave with a sense of purpose and a clear understanding of their responsibilities?

_____ + _____   = Total

Be a perfect 10. If your meetings rate 13 or above you may be spending unprofitable time and not getting the results you want to achieve.

Questions That Keep Your Wing Tips out of Your Mouth

As soon as you make a dumb comment in a meeting, you wish you could rewind the tape. Avoid these embarrassing episodes in front of senior managers and pressuring peers by learning to ask questions rather than make comments.

Ask, "Is there a faster way to accomplish this?" rather than making a comment like, "That's the worst idea I've ever heard." Or ask, "What is the background on this issue?" rather than bursting out with, "Most companies stopped doing this five years ago."

CREATE MEMORABLE MEETINGS

Both leaders and participants have a stake in making meetings memorable. Use the meeting evaluation on page 193 to make your meetings more interesting and productive.

RECAP

MO: Maximize the meeting.

→ The leader and the participants both have a stake in making a meeting profitable.

→ Leaders need to organize and control and facilitate for success.

→ Participants get buy-in for their ideas before the meeting begins and build credibility with clear, concise reporting.

19

This Could Be the Beginning of a Long-Term Relationship: Job Interviews

Simply irresistible! Package yourself as an incredible asset to an employer and make a job interview the beginning of a long-term relationship. Take a refreshing look at your accomplishments and show how your talents and energies can make a difference to the employer's future.

The Formula is your road map to the interview. The difference between a presentation and an interview is the difference between golf and baseball. In golf, as in a presentation, you are in control. You must get from the tee to the hole . . . and do it directly.

In baseball, as in an interview, the pitcher (interviewer) throws you the ball. You react. Will you whiff it or will you score a run for your side? By using the Formula you have your MO (main benefit to employer) and three strongest characteristics at the ready. Preview them at the earliest opportunity ("Tell me about yourself.") Answer subsequent questions by making a point and illustrating it with an example and a result. Here's how to prepare.

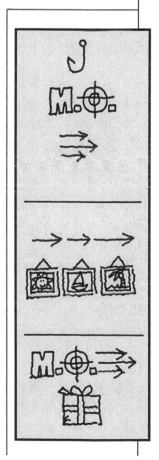

YOU ARE THE PRODUCT

Evaluate your strengths and weaknesses. What can you bring to the organization? Can you save it time or money? Can you help it work more efficiently? Can you keep the customers happy?

ORGANIZE YOUR ASSETS INTO THREE KEY POINTS

Take an inventory of your top three strengths and the benefits they offer to the "buyer." Then give specific examples to illustrate qualities such as *well-organized, dependable,* and *able to develop relationships.*

MAKE A POINT AND ILLUSTRATE IT

This step builds interest and credibility. If you want to demonstrate that you are well organized begin with:

Point: "In my last job I was responsible for three financial areas.

Illustration: "Every other month two of the three areas had payrolls due on the same day. I called in two temporaries and taught them how to handle the payrolls.

Result: "As a result, one of them became a part-time assistant and we have shortened the accounting process by one day."

Most people can easily document a point and how they handled it. It is the proof, the result of that solution, that adds impact.

Practice getting comfortable with several specific, results-oriented illustrations that sell the benefits of the product . . . *you.*

OVERCOME OBJECTIONS

Prepare to overcome your weak points with illustrations (not excuses) of how you make a handicap into an asset. When applying for a job as a Blue Cross–Blue Shield marketer, Rachel Carter turned around her lack of marketing experience by illustrating her can-do attitude and her research capabilities. She overcame the objections and won the job.

KNOW YOUR CUSTOMER

Know as much as you can about the company, its employees, and the industry where you will be interviewing. Call ahead for the printed information on the company.

Books abound with lists of common interview questions, but go on to search further. Do you know anyone in the organization? Inquire about the interviewer and get a personality reading. Try to find out if interviewers in that organization do *shock interviews* to test you in a hostile situation.

Get a friend to practice hardball, rude questioning. When a very aggressive interviewer says, "Why should we hire you over the last ten people we've talked to?" be prepared to make your point and illustrate it with specific situations and the result. Practice answering with patience, explaining your situation in a positive manner.

DEFINE THE JOB

"Get the interviewer's definition of the ideal candidate," says Bob Wilson of Wilson McLeran in his job interview workshops. The title *district manager* may have the same title as your last position, but the specific job duties could be different.

Determine the needs of the interviewer by asking questions. "Tell me about the position. What is the job like now? What would you like to see done differently in the future?"

This will not only give you insight into the job, but will allow the interviewer to talk. Most people like to talk better than listen and that's a winning relationship builder. Your interest shows that you're looking for a career fit, not just a job.

With this knowledge you can present your strengths and the specific results-oriented examples of your work in relation to the employer's requirements.

ASK FOR THE ORDER

Job interviews are sales calls. Identify the needs, demonstrate your ability to fill the job requirements, answer all the objections, then, if it's a good fit, tell the interviewer that you want to work for the organization. If there isn't a positive reply, ask for specific barriers to the opportunity. This gives you the opportunity to show how a perceived liability can be an asset.

If the interview is positive, but no job is offered, ask for a trial assignment. Johanna Costa, an accounting firm business consultant, took an assignment doing market research for a firm she was interested in before the budget was approved. During that time she had the opportunity to prove that they could not do without her.

PACKAGING IS IMPORTANT

Finally, good grooming, poised body language, confident speech, and positive mental attitude sell. The interviewer has to be sold on you as a person in order to sell you as a prospect who can represent the organization well. When we conduct interview training we turn on the camera so clients can see how they look to the interviewer.

Do an on-camera rehearsal with a friend. (See the rehearsal check sheet in chapter 15.) Do you come across as confident? Are you conversational rather then stiff? Are your responses reassuring? Have your friend role-play various types of interviewers. Do you handle negative questions patiently?

Get your personal house in order. Take a tip from real estate agencies: They urge their clients who want to sell their homes to invest in its appearance in order to make that all-important good first impression with prospects. Chipping paint, doggy odors, and messy closets get a thumbs down.

With preparation, you will come across as relaxed and confident and give the buyer the confidence that you can do the job.

EXPLORE THE FIT WITH CONFIDENCE

Think of your interview as a negotiation, not an interrogation. A young lawyer recommends assuming a peer-to-peer attitude.

"The interviewer was looking for the right person and I was looking for the right job. We interviewed each other. This attitude implies confidence. You have to be interested, but willing to walk away. If you appear desperate, the hirer will think he's getting damaged goods."

"Confidence is in your presence and your interest in the company and in the interviewer," says Lee Johnston, vice president of Human Resources for Holder Corporation, a large construction contractor. "We are looking for potential. The interviewer should be looking for the same thing."

RECAP

MO: Presence, preparation, and positive self talk, sell the benefits of *you*.

→ You are the product. Package your assets to make a difference in the prospective employer's future.

→ Know your customer.

→ Turn a handicap into an asset.

20

You Want Me
to Do *What?*
Impromptu Speaking

LEARN TO SPEAK WELL
ON A MOMENT'S NOTICE

The earth moves and your heart skips a beat. It's not romantic. It's pure panic. The minute you hear your name called for an impromptu report or response, you gasp.

Impromptu means unprepared or unplanned, an accident looking for a place to happen. It is one of the top fears our business clients talk about in workshops. The Formula is your security blanket. It will help you look good and sound confident in a spontaneous situation.

EXPECT THE UNEXPECTED

Thinking on your feet is like playing the outfield in baseball. A good player knows his position, follows the batter, and always expects the ball. Like baseball, it takes practice.

By being alert to the possibility of getting thrown into the spotlight, you will have more presence of mind. As you walk into a meeting or reception, plan your remarks. Could you be asked to give a report, toast an honoree, or introduce yourself? Ask yourself these questions: Who will be there? What's the agenda? What is my goal if I speak? What can I offer the group?

FOLLOW THE PLAY ACTION: LISTEN

The only thing worse than being called on in a meeting when you're not prepared, is being called on when you aren't listening. If you're mind tends to wander, take notes.

DEVELOP A READY RESPONSE PLAN

When you hear, "Harry, it's your turn to toast our newly promoted whiz kid," use the Formula. Pause. Quickly organize your comments into a benefit and one, two, or three points. Don't try to cover everything. Your information will be easy to follow when you have a basic framework.

Begin an unexpected report with a benefit. Then preview your key points, "In order to help you plan your schedule, let me bring you up to date on the Z project. I can report on three things: who is involved, where the budget stands, and when the project will be completed."

Give a few details on each point. Use the same technique whether someone asks you to comment on a movie, the tax bill, or your coworkers retirement.

KEEP YOUR COMMENTS SHORT

Speakers often lack confidence in their ability to express themselves, so they ramble and turn a three-minute response into a ten-minute monologue. Have the confidence to know when to end. Tangents are detours around a well-timed ending.

Personal introductions at a meeting jump-start endless mental rehearsals of the familiar. "My name is Janet Coleman, I'm a business book editor." Consider a short addition that lets the group get to know you and can jump-start future conversation. "I hail from _____" or "I'm currently editing a _____ [a book relevant to the group's interest]."

SPEAK UP

> Follow FDR's sage advice, **"Be sincere. Be brief. Be seated."**

A confident presence in an impromptu situation builds credibility. Once you determine what to say, focus on how to say it.

When you hear, "Jane, say a few words about our new vice president":

Smile to highlight your confidence.

Pause to give yourself time to think.

Sit up and forward, if you are seated, to look interested and in control.

Make eye contact so you will feel more like you are talking to one rather than many.

Power up and speak with conviction.

Keep your response focused, short. Forget whining and apologizing for your poor speaking skills. No one wants to hear excuses.

RECAP

MO: Expect the unexpected.

→ Plan ahead; stay focused on the content.

→ Keep your comments short.

→ Smile. It covers your moment of panic.

If after reading this book you have questions or would like to know more about Speechworks, write, call, fax, e-mail, or visit our Web site.

Speechworks
3353 Peachtree Road NE; Suite M30
Atlanta, GA 30326
(404) 266-0888
(404) 364-3490 (Fax)
spchwks@netdepot.com (E-mail)
www.speech-works.com (Web site)

Appendix A

How to Cure a Common Case of Cold Feet (and Other Manifestations of Nervousness)

Sir Laurence Olivier was said to throw up before every opening. *Nervous is normal*. It is fear of the unknown; it is that still, small voice in each of us that shrieks, "I'll forget what I want to say." Or, "I'll mumble." Or, "I'll embarrass myself." Or, "I'm going to be awful." Once a fear grabs hold of you, you can successfully blow it up into a huge, self-defeating block.

PHYSIOLOGICAL MANIFESTATIONS OF NERVOUSNESS AND HOW TO CONTROL THEM

Butterflies   Eat lightly before a presentation; drink water without ice.

Dry Mouth   Bite your tongue! It will cause you to salivate.

High Voice   Breathe and drop your jaw to relax the voice muscle. Practice speaking out loud with a pencil

	between your teeth to strengthen the laryngeal muscles and lower a high-pitched voice.
Knocking Knees	Have your presentation videotaped. You will see that the shaking does not show. Expect and accept the situation and persevere.
Mind Blanks	Make eye contact. Your eyes may be grazing over people's heads and taking in distracting images. Talk to one individual in the audience at a time, giving each one a thought or idea, two to three seconds. And breathe! Blanking can be caused by a deprivation of oxygen to the brain.
Not Impressive	Don't try to impress. The goal is to connect and to put your audience at ease. Jettison the jargon: Ronald Reagan spoke to the members of his audience as if they were his neighbors.
Opening Jitters	Know your easy opening line cold. Say it with power. Or start with a question and get audience response. Or hold up a prop. Focus on it to open the talk.
Peer Ridicule	Take a risk and take the lead! Risk-taking is a show of leadership. Prepare. Speak with conviction, sincerity, and enthusiasm. Those who feel that dynamic is dangerous and boring is better will neither ruffle feathers nor connect with the audience.
Pounding Heart	Valsalva maneuver. See the description of this exercise in Chapter 6, "Turn Presentation Panic into Presentation Power."
Raging Blush	This physiological condition affects TV personality Deborah Norville. Just be grateful you have high color and are not a pale flower. Wear a pink shirt to minimize the condition.

Rocking	Use the nervous energy that causes you to shift your weight to move. Take a few steps. Use your body. Emphasize important points with firm gestures. Behind the podium John F. Kennedy is said to have controlled his rocking problem by standing on the outsides of his shoes!
Shaky Hands	Dig a thumbnail deep into your palm. Hold it for a few moments. When you stop, the hand will relax and you can hold a prop or pointer without shaking.
Shaky Voice	Pause, take a breath, and deliver your well-planned, rehearsed opening with conviction. It will push you through the shaky voice phase at the beginning of a presentation.
Short of Breath	The result of shallow breathing from the chest. Breathe deeply from the abdomen. Take a breath before you begin. Pause and breathe at the end of a thought.
Sweaty Palms	Have a handkerchief in your pocket.
Talk Too Fast	You are not talking too fast, you are racing from sentence to sentence in your haste to finish. *Pause!* Breathe and count silently to three at the end of a thought. Put *pause* stickers on your notes.

Appendix B

Using the Formula: Seminar Presentation

This is an outline of a seminar given by management consultants from Kurt Salmon Associates (KSA) at an industry conference. KSA created the scenario, and its client, a national monthly magazine, told about its experience in dealing with the change process.

This seminar demonstrates the use of the Formula with subpoints in a 45 minute presentation. The subject is managing change in a cost-effective and timely manner.

Kurt Salmon Associates' consultants speak over 50 times a year, often with a client. At these conferences, they share their expertise and they build relationships that build business.

KSA SEMINAR OUTLINE

Take out four letters to form a word:

U W O T R O R L T T R   (WOOL)

Take out four letters to form a word:

T B O A N G A L N A   (BANANA)

Paradigm shift: The need to look at things differently and make necessary change for growth and success.

KSA SEMINAR OUTLINE (*Continued*)

By executing change effectively, you will save time and money.

1. Plan the change.

2. Communicate the change.

3. Manage the change.

---

1. Plan the change.
   a. Technological change
   b. Managerial change
   c. Organization change

---

a. *Planning technological change*
Plan one key implementation step months before your business deadline.

Example: Implement client-server-based magazine subscription system.

b. *Planning managerial change*
   ✔ During the transition to new management, decide who will be responsible for day-to-day management.
   ✔ Have the outgoing manager involved in training the new manager.

Example: Transition from eleven experienced managers to one experienced manager who leads seven inexperienced managers.

c. *Planning organization change*
Plan a change in staffing to encourage acceptance of technology.

Example: Transition from 800 full-time employees to 400 full-time employees.

KSA SEMINAR OUTLINE (*Continued*)

Point 1 Recap: Planning
- **a.** Technological
- **b.** Managerial
- **c.** Organization

2. Communicate the change.
- **a.** Plan your communication
- **b.** Build in redundancy
- **c.** Prepare the messenger

- **a.** *Plan communication*
  Detailed plan: dependencies and draft documents.

  Example: How the magazine communicated the procedural changes.

- **b.** *Build in redundancy*
  Tell, tell, tell—be repetitive.

  Example: Describe a work team launch.

- **c.** *Prepare the messenger*
  Develop a Q&A list for major communication points.

  Example: (Q&A prep). Magazine development and rehearsal of Q&A to support a program.

Point 2 Recap: Communicate the change.
- **a.** Plan your communication
- **b.** Build in redundancy
- **c.** Prepare the messenger

3. Manage the change.
- **a.** Start a fire
- **b.** Reward the firefighters

KSA SEMINAR OUTLINE (*Continued*)

a. *Start a fire*
Build a burning platform. *Jump in the water or go down with the platform.*

Example: Set goals and track performance of mission targeting.

b. *Reward firefighters*
Prevent backsliding by rewarding employees for continuing improvement.

Example: Implement procedural change. One operator runs two remittance processing machines.

No reward = backsliding

Reward = reinforces change

Point 3 Recap: Manage the change.

   a. Start a fire

   b. Reward the firefighters

 Execute change effectively to survive and profit.

1. Plan the change.

 2. Communicate the change.

3. Manage the change.

 Bottom-line result.

Appendix C

Using the Formula: Introducing the Speaker

Use the Formula to create an effective introduction. Attorney Horace Sibley Sr., partner of King & Spalding, introduced A. D. Frazier, the executive director of the 100th Olympiad. His Hook was the situation that brought A. D. Frazier to the Olympics. His tasks were the points of the presentation and one specific example of his accomplishments described why he was worth listening to.

Introduction of A. D. Frazier Jr. to the Atlanta Rotary Club—Monday, April 15, 1996

Imagine this scene: It's exactly five years ago. You are 47 years old. You are Executive Vice President of First Chicago Bank with national responsibility. You have successfully completed college and law school at your state university—the University of North Carolina; had a successful career at the C&S National Bank in Atlanta; headed the team which organized President Jimmy Carter's White House and Executive Office and you are serving the Chicago community on a number of high profile Boards, including Evanston Hospital, the local Public Broadcasting Corporation, Northwestern University, the Museum of Science and History, the Lyric Opera. In short, you are happy as a clam and still on your way up.

Introduction of A. D. Frazier Jr. to the Atlanta Rotary Club—Monday, April 15, 1996 (*Continued*)

Suddenly here comes a dreamy eyed lawyer from Atlanta and asks you to put on the Olympics Atlanta has just won. He says it's a great deal—you'll love it—you can pursue the Greek ideals of harmonizing body, mind and spirit and bringing the nations of the world together in friendship.

All you have to do is raise $1.5 billion dollars more or less, build or acquire and operate approximately 30 sports facilities and employ and manage around 60,000 employees and volunteers. You'll be in charge of *Finance and Administration, Operations, Olympic Programs, Sports, Capital projects and Construction.*

And, by the way, you've got five years to do the job and there's no commitment you'll have a job after the Games.

A. D.'s Leadership

 That's the scene and, of course, the guy was A. D. Frazier. And how lucky we are that A. D. Frazier took a big risk and rose to another huge challenge.

You could not find a better manager for a complex project and organization.

➞ A. D. has been able to mold a diverse group of managers and volunteers into a highly motivated and effective organization.

➞ From the beginning, A. D. set a clear vision of a financially sound private organization to produce by far the largest Olympics ever, on time and within budget.

➞ He quickly established logical functions, chose strong expert managers and set clear, achievable goals and deadlines.

Introduction of A. D. Frazier Jr. to the Atlanta Rotary Club—Monday, April 15, 1996 (*Continued*)

In one example of his success, A. D. personally negotiated many of the major contracts required for a successful Olympics, including the stadium agreement with the Braves, a $100,000,000 broadcast rights sale to Japanese Broadcasting and the recently completed Cities Services Agreement. All the while, he personally has had to attend to a swirl of external interests, including labor, various minority groups, the disabled and various levels of political bodies. A. D. has guided a new organization over and around untold shores and rough waters, under a stronger ethics code than any of our organizations has heard of and with the most successful equal economic opportunity effort in the country. To be successful, he has had to work almost every day for the past five years—days that begin at 6:00 A.M. and often end at midnight.

Atlanta simply could not have a more brilliant, skilled and dedicated person leading the Olympic operations.

It, therefore, gives me special pleasure to present to you a true Olympic hero—A. D. Frazier.

Index